LILLIAN TOO

FORTUNE

D0232641

MONKEY
2013

KONSEPBOOKS
ASTROLOGY . FENG SHUI . INSPIRATIONS

Congratulations!

Do you have what it takes to become a millionaire?
Will you be happier and healthier in 2013?
How will you look and feel? Will you marry this year?

Today I want to congratulate you and thank you
for investing in yourself. By purchasing the latest edition of
Fortune & Feng Shui, your personalized horoscope book for
2013, you now have in your possession a guide that will help
you safely through the upcoming year.

In this little book, Jennifer and I reveal many insights
pertaining to your particular animal sign… what you can
expect and how to protect and enhance all areas of your life
in 2013. Now all you need to do is to read it carefully
and take action!

And That's Just the Start!

Now you can discover more powerful secrets of feng shui
from me that go hand in hand with the valuable information
inside this little book! And it's absolutely FREE!

Won't You Join Me?

I'd like to extend my personal invitation to you to join my
FREE weekly newsletter… Lilllian Too's Mandala Ezine.

This ezine is now available in English and in Spanish!
You already took the first positive step to success by purchasing this book. Now you can expand your wealth luck and knowledge with authentic feng shui tips and advice that really work. It's like having me, Lillian Too, sitting in your office or home ready to give you my own advice, offer or strategy every week!

Don't delay! Just go to *www.lilliantoomandalaezine.com* and register today! You'll receive my ezine in your inbox every Wednesday loaded with valuable tips and feng shui articles to make 2013 your best year ever!

It's FREE! It's NEW! It's EASY TO USE!
GENUINE FENG SHUI TIPS AND
ARTICLES EVERY WEEK!

Sign up for your FREE copy right now and judge for yourself how much it's worth to you! Go to:
www.lilliantoomandalaezine.com
And Hurry! When you register today, you'll also receive a FREE special BONUS from me.
This offer is good for a limited time… so hurry!

All the best,
Lillian

P.S. Lillian's online FREE weekly ezine is only available to those who register online at *www.lilliantoomandalaezine.com*

P.P.S. Ezine subscribers also receive special offer, discounts and bonuses from me throughout the year!

Fortune & Feng Shui 2013 MONKEY
by Lillian Too and Jennifer Too
© 2013 Konsep Lagenda Sdn Bhd

Text © 2013 Lillian Too and Jennifer Too
Photographs and illustrations © WOFS.com Sdn Bhd

The moral right of the authors to be identified as authors of this book has
been asserted.

Published by KONSEP LAGENDA SDN BHD (223 855)
Kuala Lumpur 59100 Malaysia

For more Konsep books, go to www.lillian-too.com or www.wofs.com
To report errors, please send a note to errors@konsepbooks.com
For general feedback, email feedback@konsepbooks.com

ISBN 978-967-329-095-6
Published in Malaysia, August 2012

THE MONKEY

This is the sign most often associated with quick wit, great inner wisdom and possessed of the ability to amass great wealth. Remember the three W's – wit, wisdom and wealth – brought together and actualized into practical reality by a mind as quick as lightning! This describes the sign of the Monkey. You learn quickly, you adapt fast and you move with the kind of speed that leaves those close to you gasping to keep up. As a young woman, you are an atrocious flirt, and as a young man, people will describe you as a playboy. But this is because the Monkey gets bored with those unable to appreciate your creativity or your new ideas or your moving from one subject to the next.

The mature Monkey may move with less speed, but is nevertheless as bright and as quick. As a result, in work situations, the Monkey can come across insensitive and unfeeling. It is easy for you to aggravate those who are mentally challenged. But the Monkey is so good natured and rarely if ever gets into an angry state of mind, so the Monkey sign is usually also a popular sign. People find it impossible to stay cross with you as you can also be extremely charming and endearing. You are generous to a fault and you rarely gossip about others. You are extremely positive, always seeing the nice side of people, as a result of which you exude good natured vibes.

But the Monkey born is also very independent and you will want to do things your way. You are also a high achiever and challenges excite you and give you an adrenaline rush. You are a keen competitor; in whatever you undertake, you will train, you will learn and you will practice. Indeed, you harbour a secret ambition to be a super hero – somewhere within your inner psyche lies the conviction that you are operating at only ten percent of your real capability. Thus the Monkey never stops striving or aiming for the highest skies

MONKEY *Born Chart*

BIRTH YEAR	WESTERN CALENDAR DATES	AGE	KUA NUMBER MALES	KUA NUMBER FEMALES
WOOD Monkey	25 Jan 1944 to 12 Feb 1945	69	2 West Group	4 East Group
FIRE Monkey	12 Feb 1956 to 30 Jan 1957	57	8 West Group	7 West Group
EARTH Monkey	30 Jan 1968 to 16 Feb 1969	45	5 West Group	1 East Group
METAL Monkey	16 Feb 1980 to 4 Feb 1981	33	2 West Group	4 East Group
WATER Monkey	4 Feb 1992 to 22 Jan 1993	21	8 West Group	7 West Group
WOOD Monkey	22 Jan 2004 to 8 Feb 2005	9	5 West Group	1 East Group

CONTENTS

CONTENTS

PART 5.
Improving Monkey's Feng Shui in 2013

CONTENTS

PART ONE

SNAKE YEAR 2013
A Year with Sustenance Luck

LUCK OF THE
WATER SNAKE YEAR 2013
A Year with Sustenance Luck

The **Water Snake** brings a fresh set of energies to the
new year and looking at the Feng Shui and Paht Chee
charts that define the year's energies, two significant
things stand out; one is that the feng shui square of
2013 brings us back to the original **Lo Shu with 5 in the
center**. This happens every nine years and indicates that
all 12 signs essentially get strongly influenced by their
original essence. Both their series of **Element Luck
indications** as well as each of their ruling **Trigrams**
exerts strong influences on their fortunes in 2013. The
second significant revelation is that the year's **Paht
Chee** chart continues the improving trend in element
combinations we have been seeing since last year.

The Paht Chee Chart of 2013 is well balanced with
all five elements present - there are 2 Water, 2 Earth, 2
Wood, 1 Metal and 1 Fire. This suggests a year when
everyone has the chance to see better times during the
year. Disasters - natural or manmade - are significantly
subdued. A new sense of calm pervades the year. Unlike
the previous year, which saw political changes and
upheavals in many countries, this coming year will see a
time of consolidation. People will refocus their goals.

And while older folk will try to bring attention back to wealth creation and strengthening of the previous old order, the younger generation, who currently carry the mood of the world, will increasingly focus their attention on finding new ways of achieving their goals. This difference in focus will see additional breakthroughs taking place in the discovery of new technology organizing our lives. How the people of the world interact with each other, how we work, communicate and disseminate information will continue to bring big changes into the world, and the results are not necessarily bad.

But note that 2013 signifies the beginning of the second half of the Period of 8.

The influence of 8 is at its height with the number 5 ruling the energies of the world. The number 8 is back in its home location of Northeast, so the *young man* continues to exert strong influence on the world's environment – whether for good or for ill.

The Paht Chee shows that the year is defined by the **Yin Metal element** which is neither strong nor weak. It is auspicious that in the **Day Pillar**, Yin Earth produces Yin Metal. There is thus **sustenance luck** this year.

In 2013 there are only two clashing pillars; clashes happen in the **Year Pillar**, where Yin Water puts out the Yin Fire of Snake, and in the **Hour Pillar**, where Yang Earth overcomes the Yang Water of Rat.

In the YEAR pillar, the heavenly stem of Yin Water puts out the Earthly branch of Yin Snake. This reduces the Snake's Vitality for the year. There is also only a single Fire element in the chart, and Fire signifies rank, power and status this year. What this clash in the Year pillar suggests is that intelligence, mental capability and creativity will overcome the raw use of power during the year. It is a year when those who are clever will do much better than those who are in positions of power, irrespective of their status or place in society. This clash does not bring negative results or influences to the year.

In the HOUR pillar, the heavenly stem of Yang Earth, which represents strong resource luck, subdues the Yang Water of Rat. Here we have seen that Water stands for intelligence this year, so towards the end of the year, it is Resources that counts more than Intelligence. This is a time when the heavenly stem prevails.

The two clashing pillars therefore need not be feared.

Meanwhile, there are many hidden elements that strengthen the year's core energies, in particular the Yin Metal of the year's essence. Note also that the excellent presence of **Rat and Ox together** in the chart generates **additional Yang Earth**, which adds to the Resource Luck of the year. This contributes to the luck of goodwill in the international environment. Diplomacy exerts a dominant role in relations between countries, and the energy of hostility is reduced.

With the Internet bringing people into greater communication with one another, this is a very welcome indication. The year should also witness more **friendly alliances** taking place and there is greater evidence of cooperation that has been missing in the recent past years. The most important indicator of positive readings is the presence of all five elements. 2013 is an environment when goodwill can take seed and grow.

The presence and ready availability of Resource Luck supports continued improvement in the economies of the world. The outlook is thus a lot better than in previous years.

The sign of the Rat features in the Paht Chee chart in the Hour Pillar, and next to it in the Day Pillar is the Ox. This creates the Rat and Ox secret friend and soulmate alliance in the chart. Their presence in the year's Paht Chee is extremely beneficial for the year,

2013 *Paht Chee Chart*

YEAR OF THE WATER SNAKE			
HOUR	**DAY**	**MONTH**	**YEAR**
HEAVENLY STEM	HEAVENLY STEM	HEAVENLY STEM	HEAVENLY STEM
戊	辛	甲	癸
YANG EARTH	YIN METAL	YANG WOOD	YIN WATER
EARTHLY BRANCH	EARTHLY BRANCH	EARTHLY BRANCH	EARTHLY BRANCH
壬 子	己 丑	甲 寅	丁 巳
YANG WATER intelligence RAT	YIN EARTH resources OX	YANG WOOD wealth luck TIGER	YIN FIRE power SNAKE
HIDDEN ELEMENTS			
RAT & OX BRING YANG EARTH RESOURES	YIN METAL YIN WATER	YANG EARTH YANG FIRE	YANG EARTH YANG METAL

SPECIAL STARS: POWERFUL MENTORS AND SCHOLASTIC BRILLIANCE

because it suggests close affinity in the astrological stakes. This suggests a strengthening of goodwill, tolerance and affinity luck for the year. This does not happen often.

The year is meanwhile blessed with two auspicious stars making an appearance – the *Star of Scholastic Brilliance* and the *Star of Powerful Mentors*.

The **Star of Scholastic Brilliance** is created by the presence of the Yin Metal in the Day Pillar interacting with the Rat in the Hour Pillar.

This Star benefits all kinds of intellectual pursuits and there will also be a trend towards the pursuit of knowledge. Discoveries of the mind will bring satisfaction and a sense of achievement to those engaged in such work; research and creativity will be nurtured this year and the developing of new expertise becomes a trendy pursuit. There is recognition from high levels.

The year's Paht Chee also has the presence of the *Powerful Mentors Star.* In Chinese, this is the luck of the *Gui Ren*, helpful patrons who play the role of mentor to young protégés. This will manifest at the work place, in schools and in colleges. This is one of the most valuable kinds of luck to have, and it is definitely beneficial to activate it for your private benefit. The presence of this star suggests that those in positions of authority tend to be kinder and more tolerant in their attitude towards those under their supervision or care, and less authoritative. There will not be so much bullying.

This star is also known as the *Heavenly Virtue Star* and it predicts the compassionate attitude of people in power will manifest more; so they use their influence to help others. It is an excellent indication for the year as it is this star which will bring greater happiness and less cause for suffering.

> The presence of this positive *Heavenly Virtue Star* augurs well for the continuation of recovery prospects and advancement outlooks for many of the world's economies this year.

It is an interesting phenomenon that in 2013, it is the year's ruling animal sign i.e. the Snake together with the Yin Metal of the Day Pillar which is creating this *Powerful Mentors Star*. This suggests that this is a benevolent Snake Year. From a spiritual feng shui aspect, it also suggests that the nagas or *Spirits of the Earth* will be helpful rather than destructive. This is further confirmed by Earth producing Metal in the Day Pillar.

When the Earth Spirits of the year are helpful in this manner, there is a higher probability of peace and prosperity prevailing. When the Earth spirits are in wrathful mode, they tend to be destructive, causing disasters, poor harvests and earth-related problems to manifest. From a Tibetan astrological viewpoint, the nagas of the year are in helpful mode. This is a relief, because in a Snake Year, *naga power* is significant.

WHAT THE ELEMENTS MEAN IN 2013'S CHART

Each year the five elements signify different types of luck, and it is always a good sign when all five elements make an appearance in the chart. With no element missing, the year's outlook will be balanced, bringing harmony and fewer problems and obstacles.

WEALTH LUCK is represented by the element of **WOOD** and with two of these in the main chart, there is definitely the presence of new wealth getting created during the year. Prosperity opportunities are certain to materialize for those who are on the lookout. There is **no hidden Wood** in the chart, so all Wealth luck comes directly.

Those born in the year of the Monkey belong to the element of Metal so your intrinsic element controls the Wood element. This suggests that your success luck potential in the area of wealth creation is extremely strong. This is also born out in your Elements chart, which shows a strong and powerful lung ta or Wind Horse. Those of you born in the year of the Monkey are thus seeing a potentially great year ahead in terms of success in wealth creation. For you, wealth luck is most promising during the months of **February** and **November.**

RESOURCE LUCK this year is represented by the element of **EARTH**. There is more than enough of this element in this year's chart with one direct Yang Earth and one direct Yin Earth. In addition, there are four **Yang Earth** elements that are hidden. So directly and indirectly, there is **plenty of resource availability**.

This year's intrinsic element is **Yin Metal**, which indicates that all good fortune and all categories of good luck will manifest easily. This is probably the best news for the year. Earth ensures that the intrinsic Metal energy of the year is kept constantly nourished. The resource availability situation is just so good! Any danger this year comes from there being too much Earth. When there is excess of any element, it can create imbalances.

The clever balancing of elements in your living space is always a key factor to address, as this is what attracts and sustains good fortune so it might be a good idea to increase the presence of metal energy in your homes and offices. This should soak up the excess Earth although for the Monkey whose intrinsic element is Metal all the surplus Earth energy is not bad at all since Earth produces Metal. For you also Earth strengthens your Life Force and Inner Essence so the surplus Earth is excellent for you.

It is beneficial in 2013 to wear gold & for there to be windchimes hanging in the Earth sectors of the home i.e. SOUTHWEST (the sector that signifies your vitality) & NORTHEAST (the sector which signifies your personal power).

POWER LUCK in 2013 is represented by the element of **FIRE** which is present in the main chart as **Yin Fire**. There is also one hidden **Yang Fire**. This indicates there is a good balance of authority luck. That there is both direct and hidden Fire suggests that the year does not lack the luck of rank and authority. This means that the rule of law will not be compromised. However, the presence of Fire is in the Year pillar, and this means that power energy comes at the very start of the year and will likely be in the hands of older and wiser people. The year favours power exercised by the older generation in the family.

ENHANCER: If you want to enhance your personal power, increase the voltage of light in the **Northeast** sector of your home or office. An excellent idea is to have a **table lamp** or a lamp featuring **radiating lights** in this corner of your desk or work table. Using LED lights this way works very well. This will add greatly to your personal power and is extremely effective for those seeking promotion or upward mobility.

FRIENDSHIP LUCK looks good for the year and this is signified by the element of **METAL** in 2013. There is a single **Yin Metal** in the main chart, but this is strongly supported by one hidden **Yin Metal** and one hidden **Yang Metal**. More significantly, there is more than enough Earth to keep Metal strong. The analysis of this situation is that there will be good friendship luck during the year, and friends may start out genuine and sincere, but it will be all too easy for jealousy to set in.

ENHANCER: If you want magnify friendship luck in 2013 i.e. you want more friends, or a busier social life with more friendship overtures coming your way, hang the **Four Friends Windchime** that feature the double happiness and special mystical knot symbols in the **West** sector of your homes. These have varying degrees of intensity which attract from casual platonic friendships to intense love relationships.

💧 **INTELLIGENCE LUCK** in 2013 is represented by the element of **WATER**. There is a single showing of this element in the year's chart and it is signified the Rat earthly branch in the Hour pillar. This means that the best ideas and the highest creativity come from young people and they will be most inspired to show their visionary abilities towards the end of the year.

> **ENHANCER:** To stimulate greater brain power and creativity in 2013, the best enhancer is to place a **small water feature** near you. Using the Water element to stimulate your brain cells is not the same as using Water to attract wealth luck. Here, what is excellent is to simulate water seeping up from the earth and flowing smoothly down a large stone representing Earth energy.

FLYING STAR NUMBERS OF 2013

The 2013 Feng Shui grid shown here is the easiest and most popular way to understand the fundamental feng shui energy pattern of the year. The numbers that "fly" into each of the compass sectors reveal how chi congregates within any built-up structure.

Usually, Feng Shui practitioners superimpose the nine numbers of the year's chart onto the floor plans of homes and offices to get a good idea of the dominant number in each of the eight main sectors of the home.

The numbers 1 to 9 reveal the luck of sectors, corners and rooms in the home or office. Every level of the building is affected by the way the numbers move around inside it, so the grid of numbers are superimposed on every floor level. Each number has its own energy which can be auspicious or unlucky. The numbers offer a snapshot of the luck patterns of the different compass sectors of the home.

Most feng shui practitioners can easily differentiate the afflictive from the auspicious numbers and there are effective ways of subduing the bad numbers and of manifesting the lucky numbers. For those of you new to feng shui, this is basically how the feng shui of homes are updated and improved each year.

The Flying Star feng shui chart of 2013 is dominated by the powerful five yellow or **wu wang** and this means that the chart for this Year of the Snake is the original Lo Shu magic square.

SE	SOUTH	SW
TAI SUI		**ILLNESS**
4	**9**	**2**
HOSTILE	**WU WANG**	**VIOLENCE**
3	**5**	**7**
POWERFUL	**VICTORY**	**AUSPICIOUS**
8	**1**	**6**
NE	NORTH	NW

EAST (left side)　WEST (right side)

This implies that each of the nine numbers of the Flying Star chart exerts a very strong influence on the energies of their respective sectors, simply because they are in their original position. Element-wise, there is neither a weakening nor a strengthening of any of the nine numbers.

Activating the auspicious star numbers and suppressing the negative numbers makes up an important aspect of updating the time dimension feng shui of any building or built-up space.

This year is not any different, so the first thing to do to update your feng shui to ensure a continuation of good fortune luck is to activate the good fortune areas.

> In 2013, the **good luck sectors** of the year are **North, Northwest** and **Northeast** because these are the three sectors with the auspicious white star numbers 1, 6 and 8, with 8 being the most auspicious.

In addition, the sectors **South** with the 9 and **East** with the 4 can also be regarded as positive numbers. Activating them will also attract their dimension of good fortune. There are three ways to activate energy i.e. make it move, thereby energizing its intrinsic meanings to manifest. This encourages yang chi to come alive. Good feng shui thus requires us to use either one of the three ways of creating good yang chi in the auspicious sectors of the home:

Firstly, create noise – keep the radio or television turned on in the sector with auspicious numbers. In 2013, this method can be used to energize the white numbers 1, 6 and 8 in the **North**, **Northwest** and **Northeast**. Houses facing these directions benefit very much from these numbers.

Secondly, create movement - organize the sitting areas where people congregate e.g. place your sofa sets and tables in sectors that have lucky numbers. The presence of people generates **human energy**, which is always the most powerful when it comes to activating the chi.

Thirdly, create bright light - place lamps or bring sunshine into corners of your home or living room that you want to energize during the year.

Each time any space is activated in any of these three ways, the number that occupies the space gets activated, so using any of these methods would be effective feng shui ways of generating good energies in the home. However, it is also important to ensure that sounds, movement, activity and lights should also be substantially reduced in the sectors that are occupied by negative numbers.

DEALING WITH THE 5 IN THE CENTER

The center of the square this year is occupied by the five yellow, which is regarded as a misfortune star.

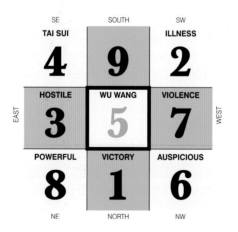

Its location in the center of the chart indicates that if you are unlucky enough to get hit by its misfortune luck phenomena, the consequences can be serious. The *wu wang* 5 is generally feared by many Feng Shui Masters. This is something which everyone must be aware of and prepared for. There are those however for whom the number 5 not only does not present any danger, but who stand to benefit from the 5 being in the dominating center position of the chart.

The table here shows the men and women who benefit from the number 5 being in the center.

MEN who benefit from center 5	WOMEN who benefit from center 5
SNAKE (born 1941)	RAT (born 1936)
TIGER (born 1950)	ROOSTER (born 1945)
BOAR (born 1959)	HORSE (born 1954)
EARTH MONKEY (born 1968)	RABBIT (born 1963)
SNAKE (born 1977)	RAT (born 1972)
TIGER (born 1986)	ROOSTER (born 1981)
BOAR (born 1995)	HORSE (born 1990)
WOOD MONKEY (born 2004)	RABBIT (born 1999)
SNAKE (born 2013)	RAT (born 2008)

Note that the Gentleman Earth Monkey born in 1968 and the Wood Monkey born in 2004 benefit from the 5 in the centre in 2013.

These individuals should enjoy continued improvement of their previous year's good fortune; i.e. if the Dragon Year of 2012 brought you good fortune, this luck will continue to expand with no hindrance. If the previous year brought you bad luck however, the 5 in the center will suppress all further bad luck.

This phenomenon applies to **Men born in the Monkey years of 1968 and 2004**. For all others not in the table, the 5 in the center is bad news as it indicates that there is the possibility of danger and misfortune befalling them or their homes and work places. It can manifest as illness, accident or loss of wealth and profits. Those born in Monkey year including **all Female Monkeys** who do not benefit from the 5, must be wary of the 5 in the center.

Misfortune brought by the number 5 *wu wang* star can manifest as illness, accident or loss of wealth and profits.

For all of you, the number 5 must NOT be energized or made strong in any way. This means keep the center of homes or rooms less brightly lit. Lights or Fire energy will always strengthen the 5.

Note that the number 5 is an Earth number, and there is plenty of hidden Earth energy already in 2013, as revealed by the year's Paht Chee chart. This tells us that the afflictive strength of the 5 is already very strong this year.

The danger of the 5 flaring up is that it could bring a whole series of bad news, illness, obstacles to success and all kinds of depressing feelings. An aura of despondency can get created unless it is suppressed. For everyone, it is advisable to look out for the month when the number 5 travels to your animal sign sector, because that is the month when the 5's affliction strength is directed at your sign.

For the Monkey born, the number 5 flies to your home location of Southwest in May, so if 5 is harmful to you, please make sure you put the cures in place by then.

Unless you display the correct cure, the month of May could be quite a trial and definitely will be very aggravating indeed and you might well succumb to misfortune luck. Remember that the afflictions of 5 strike unexpectedly, causing sudden problems to manifest.

Meanwhile for those of you in business, note that the year **does not** have a *lap chun*, suggesting there could be cash flow problems causing you some worry. The lack of a *lap chun* combined with the 5 in the center can cause finances to become unstable.

7-LEVEL PAGODA

Afflictions brought by the number 5 in the center of the chart affects all sectors of the home. They must be suppressed by the presence of either a suitably filled **7-level Pagoda** or a **special Stupa** which contains powerful sacred syllables and incantations. The 7-level pagoda made of chrome gold metal decorated with the Dragon naga is especially excellent for ensuring that whatever Earth energy is activated does not bring problems. This pagoda is especially **beneficial** for homes with **young children** still in school, as it not only protects them from misfortune but also improves their concentration and helps them do better at school and in examinations.

KALACHAKRA STUPA

For greater power and to bring in the radiance of uplifting energy to counter the despondency blues of the center 5, an even more powerful cure is the **Kalachakra Stupa** which resembles the popular **5-Element Pagoda**. It is however far more colourful, reflecting the 5 elements, and is associated with the powerful legendary **King of Shambhala**, who is linked with the Kalachakra tradition that governs the **Wheel of Time.**

Displaying this particular Stupa in the home ensures protection against evil forces and also **attracts big wealth luck.** Good things can literally fall from the sky! It is exceedingly lucky to invite this meaningful Stupa into your home in 2013 because Snake Years activate the *Earth nagas*, and since this is the year of the peaceful Snake, it is a good time to slip this Stupa into the home to generate powerful radiating energies, hence transforming the Earth nagas into your cosmic allies.

PAIR OF WALKING CAMELS

Those in business and in need of a remedy to counter the possibility of being hit by **cash flow problems** will find it helpful to display **a pair of walking camels**. Single-humped camels are used for stabilizing finances and safeguarding wealth, while the double-humped Camels symbolize overcoming financial difficulties and cash flow problems. Camels have also been used to counter the absence of the *lap chun*, and in 2013, the lap chun is missing because the Lunar New Year date comes after February 4th.

In 2013, the presence of the **Kalachakra Stupa** with a **pair of camels** are the two symbols that bring the most beneficial feng shui. These subdue the afflictions of the number 5, and attract good fortune simultaneously. Note that our Kalachakra Stupas contain sacred seed syllables, powerful sutra texts and enhancing mantras that actualize the fervent wishes of the residents of the household. We also add **wishfulfilling jewels** into the body of the Stupa to further increase their potency.

ENHANCING THE NUMBER 6 IN THE NORTHWEST

In 2013, the number 6 flies into the **Northwest**. This Big Metal number flying into its home location brings big benefits to the Patriarch of the home. The male father figure should thus make the fullest use of this year's good fortune energies. The Northwest is where the chi of heaven usually accumulates, and in 2013, there are also two auspicious stars brought by the 24 Mountains into this sector of the compass as well.

This sector of the home must thus be strongly activated with powerful **metallic windchimes** that

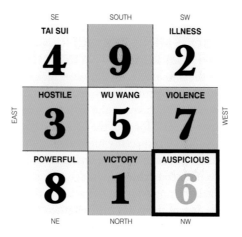

are suitably embellished with the energizing symbols. Movement of the chimes activates the symbols, which then resonate with the 6 in this sector to bring the good fortune implied in the symbols.

ACTIVATING SYMBOL
FOR THE NORTHWEST:

The best way to activate the energies of the Northwest is to have something here which will get the energy moving. It is **movement** that creates the cause for energy to move, thereby transforming it into powerful yang chi. This is exactly what is needed to benefit the father of the household. We thus recommend the following enhancer custom-made for 2013.

PRECIOUS MINISTER 'QUI REN'
HOLDING A RU YI AND WINDCHIME

directs the *Star of Powerful Mentors* luck to the Northwest sector. The Monkey will find it very beneficial to activate the manifestation of a mentor because for you, the luck of success through 2013 is especially high already, so having a mentor will maximize this luck tremendously. You do not need extra help in this category of luck, but using feng shui to activate the *Mentor Star* of the year can strengthen your success potential further. Do this by inviting the **Precious Minister** in the Northwest sector. This will attract the kind of support which assists you to become more upwardly mobile, especially those of you in a career or professional situation. It will bring powerful new influences into your working life! When you invite this nobleman, look closely and you will see that the Minister is holding a **Ru Yi** in one hand and a **Windchime** in the other.

ACTIVATING THE 1 IN THE NORTH

The Victory Star 1 flies to the North in 2013 and it brings good fortune and quick success luck to all those whose bedrooms are located in this sector. The number 1 is an auspicious white number, and the North is its original location. It is strong and robust and does not need much strengthening, but it *does* need to be activated.

ACTIVATORS FOR THE NORTH: The best way to keep the chi moving in this location is to use its own element i.e. Water; so a table top **water feature** here is sufficient.

If your bedroom is located here and you want victory luck, you can place a **Banner of Victory** in the North corner of your room. It is not advisable to have water features in the bedroom.

In the living areas where you spend time, having a small zen-like **water bubbling up over stone feature** would be excellent. This would be especially beneficial to the young sons of the family.

ACTIVATING
THE 8 IN THE NORTHEAST

The Northeast benefits very much from the number 8 in 2013 and since this is a strong number 8 (as it is in its original position), anyone living in a Northeast facing or sitting direction house is sure to benefit.

The 8 star benefits those whose bedrooms are located in the Northeast sector, or whose homes have main doors located in their Northeast corner. Those whose bedrooms are in the Northeast should enhance the energy of 8 by placing the **Crystal 8 embedded with real gold chips** here. This enhancing symbol has been around for several years now, and continues to be powerful all through the Period of 8, which lasts until 2024.

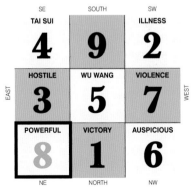

Those occupying a room in this sector can directly benefit from the powerfully potent number 8 star in the Northeast by magnifying its impact. Do this by hanging a **large 8-rod windchime** decorated with the wishfulfilling images of the sun, moon, peacock and rabbit.

To energize the 8, you can also create **a pair of wealth vases** with golden coins, gems and ingots within a crystal ball. This symbolizes the powerful wealth luck captured within the Earth element of the crystal.

If your main door is located in the Northeast, it is beneficial to install a **bright light** near the door, as Fire enhances the Earth energy of 8. It is also a good idea to keep the door opened as much as you can. This **welcomes in the energy of 8** into the home.

NURTURING
NUMBER 4 IN THE SOUTHEAST

In the lineage texts on Flying Star time dimension feng shui, the green star 4 is not an unlucky number and has absolutely no negative connotations. Instead, the green 4 represents excellent *Peach Blossom Luck* which brings love, romance and marriage opportunities to those who are eligible, single and on the lookout for romance.

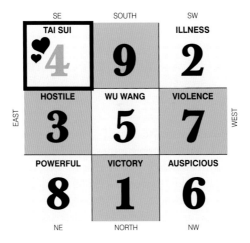

The number 4 is a Wood star, so those who have bedrooms in the Southeast need to be a mindful they do not allow their love life to get out of hand. The

Monkey's intrinsic element is Metal so there is little danger of over activating the 4 because Metal controls Wood – nevertheless, if you have too much water here, the 4 can get over-energized, resulting in infidelity luck manifesting! Water here thus can lead to sexual scandals developing. By water, we are referring to aquariums, pools and ponds. We are not referring to smaller water features that do not have accumulated water.

> Those who are happily married must be especially mindful of this, as water energizing the 4 star can sometimes lead to infidelity and moments of weakness that can lead to unhappy consequences.

Feng shui traditionalists regard 4 as the number which enhances marriage opportunities, especially for those families with eligible young men or women, and whose main entrance doors face the location occupied by it. However, when it is over-activated, it can lead to romance that goes beyond existing marriages. And for those whose bedrooms are placed in the Southeast in 2013, please be very mindful that Water energy is not inadvertently activated!

In 2013, the luck of this star number benefits those having their bedrooms located in this sector of the house. For them, this star number brings romance luck as well as the energy associated with literary and concentration. This is because the number 4 is often also respected as the *Scholar Star* that brings **good fortune to academic pursuits**.

If your family comprises children or teenagers still at school or pursuing their studies in college, nurturing the number 4 star with a **small water feature** will help assure them of good results in their studies, examinations and in their applications for admission into the College of their choice or in their search for a good start to their career.

It is however worthwhile noting that the water features used **must not be too large**, otherwise the number 4 can turn ugly, bringing the affliction of infidelity and sexual scandal. Too much water is always a dangerous thing.

CREATE YANG CHI FOR THE NUMBER 9 IN THE SOUTH

The number 9 star in 2013 is affected by both good and bad influences this year. The South sector where it is located has two auspicious stars and one star which brings loss; these are the three stars of the 24 mountains, so the luck of future prosperity looks mixed this year.

The number 9 always signifies strong magnifying energy, and it is generally regarded as second only to the number 8 in bringing good fortune and prosperity.

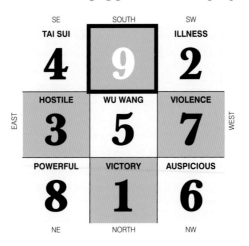

Thus it is always excellent to enhance the Fire energy of 9, because Fire reflects its intrinsic essence. And because in 2013, 9 is located in its own home location of South, its fire burns bright! In this sector, 9 is strong, so it brings the luck of harvesting which benefits those whose bedrooms or main doors are located in the South of the building. To enhance the luck and ensure it manifests prosperity and success, wear a **round jade disc with a success symbol in gold**.

Offices located in the South enjoy the **luck of planning and strategizing** for the future. If your door faces South, it is likewise beneficial this year. Keep the sector well lit as this strengthens its vitality and adds the luck of power and authority to the residents of the household.

ENHANCER FOR MAGNIFYING 9: The power of 9 is magnified when there is **movement** and **light**. This creates new yang chi which enhances the vitality of the sector. Place a **rotating red lamp** here and if there are auspicious symbols signifying wealth and success on the lamp as it rotates, the feng shui benefits are even more incredible.

SUPPRESS ILLNESS CHI OF NUMBER 2 IN THE SOUTHWEST

In 2013, the number 2 star flies back to its home location of Southwest. This also happens to be the home location of the Monkey, so all of you born in the Monkey year are vulnerable to the illness star, especially since your animal sign is also having a low reading on your Life Force luck.

The **57 year old Fire Monkey** is especially susceptible to this illness star affliction and must be extra careful this year, especially during the months of May and August.

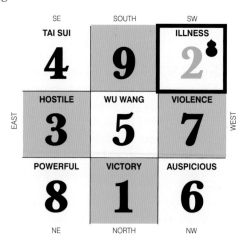

Meanwhile, because we are in the Period of 8, this number's negative side is dominant. Thus the number 2's illness vibrations to this matriarchal corner are particularly strong this year. Bedrooms or doors located here will be afflicted by illness energy, and it is generally advisable to avoid too much noise or movement in the Southwest. Too much activity here will cause problems relating to the wellness and health of the residents residing in this part of the house.

Excessively bright lighting is also not advisable. The illness star is an Earth element star, so its location in an Earth sector strengthens it. It is therefore vital to subdue this affliction; otherwise it gets stronger through the year. It is never pleasant getting sick or succumbing to the fever bug or the coughing or flu bug.

And remember that for the Monkey, you need to be extra careful because your Life Force and Spirit Essence are very low in 2013 you can easily succumb to the illness star's afflictions.

Be extra careful during the months of **May** and **August** when the numbers 5 and 2 enters into your home location of Southwest respectively.

Generally, it is a good idea to keep the illness number well subdued in the sector where it flies to each year.

The Monkey benefits from sitting on the 24 Mountains *Star of Heavenly Seal*, which indicates that you will enjoy strong support from the Heavenly Deities, but on either side of you are affliction stars that could cause you some trouble. Unhappily you have the Yin House star on your left and the *Star of Facing Three Killings* on your left and both are troublesome and even dangerous stars. Because of these various signs suggesting real afflictions befalling your health and Life Force during 2013, it is a good idea to place a longevity vase near your bed, especially if you are also having your bedroom located in the Southwest of your house.

CURE FOR ILLNESS STAR:
Make use of the **Longevity Vase** to maintain good health. The Tibetans have a great tradition for maintaining the continued good health for the older amongst them and also for their revered high lamas. This is the Longevity Vase made in silver or gold and filled with **long life mantras.**

CONTROL
THE NUMBER 7 IN THE WEST

The number 7 star brought danger to the patriarchs of the world in the previous year. This year, the 7 flies to the West, bringing danger of violence and suffering to this direction.

When we think of the West, we think usually of the United States, so there might be outbreaks of anger and things getting out of hand there. This is possible because the West is intrinsically metallic in its element essence, so the Metal energy of 7 is not weak. It is in

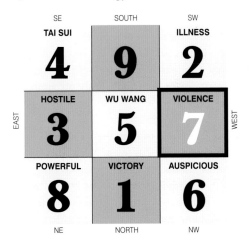

SE	SOUTH	SW
TAI SUI		**ILLNESS**
4	**9**	**2**
HOSTILE	**WU WANG**	**VIOLENCE**
3	**5**	**7**
POWERFUL	**VICTORY**	**AUSPICIOUS**
8	**1**	**6**
NE	NORTH	NW

EAST — WEST

fact quite strong and it affects the energy of the West sector inside homes - apartments as well as landed property. The danger is that the 7 can manifest robbery, rebellion or simply some kind of violence experience affecting you. The number 7 in 2013 is a red star located in a Metal element environment.

When metal and red come together, it almost always signifies physical injury caused by metal – the spilling of blood (the red 7) caused by guns, knives, swords or other kinds of weapons (metal).

The number 7 star is bad news in the current period of 8 as it also brings people with bad intentions into the direction it dominates. This suggests that the West part of a country, city or home will easily succumb to 7's malevolent energies.

It is always advisable to keep the number 7 under control. Knowing the 7 is in the West, it is a good idea to move rooms if you are either sleeping or working in a West-located room in 2013. This is a strong affliction, well worth taking some trouble over. Should one get hit by the 7 star affliction, it is a most unpleasant experience that can include being physically hurt. Mentally also, the 7 star brings betrayal and a breakdown of trust that can be very unpleasant. This star should definitely be subdued.

CURE FOR NUMBER 7: An effective way to control the 7 star is with Water energy, as Water exhausts the Metal element of the 7. Get this year's model of the **water feature that has the Rhino and Elephant in wrathful mode**. Instead of flowing water, use something with bubbling water instead, as the 7 is strong this year. Place red banners by the side with the words "wealth is safe".

SUBDUING THE
HOSTILE STAR 3 IN THE EAST

In 2013, the hostile star number 3 disturbs the peace of the East, affecting the luck of the eldest son. With the 3 here, the energy generated could cause severe conflicts between the generations in any household. Sons (especially eldest sons) and fathers will find fault with one another, incessantly disturbing the peace of the household.

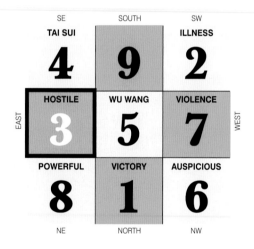

Angry mood swings afflict the energy of homes that either face or sit East, and such homes will require special feng shui remedies, otherwise there is disharmony in the household. This can also bring stress and strain to marriages and sibling relationships, and widen generational differences. This is because in the East, the number 3 star is very strong indeed. Here the Wood element can easily grow and expand, especially if there is the presence of water here.

> Bedrooms located in the East will be especially afflicted by the 3 star, and every effort must be made to suppress it. The use of bright lights that strengthen Fire energy will weaken the Wood of the 3, so anything **red in colour** will reduce the strength of the 3.

The number 3 star can also attract legal problems to your household. Court cases, litigation and severe quarrelsome energy enter homes that have prominent East sectors (e.g. when the main door is located in the East sector or is facing East) and these are sure to make life very aggravating. So if you have an East-facing door, the advice is to try using another door this year.

Try also to increase lighting to the East part of the house. This is the best remedy to weaken the 3 star.

The number 3 star will be effectively subdued when robust Fire energy is introduced to the East location of your house, so if you have nothing else, just keep this location well lit. Hostility energy instantly gets reduced.

In 2013, the East is also afflicted by the *Three Killings* affliction, so any remedy for the number 3 star should also subdue the Three Killings. We recommend these cures:

1. The **3 SUN MIRRORS**
This is a very powerful cure indeed and when placed in the East in 2013 will effectively wipe out all hostile vibes. The 3 Sun Mirrors are also effective for subduing the *Three Killings*.

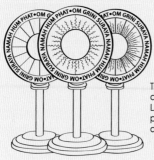

The Sun, the Bright Sun, and the Radiant Sun Light up your career prospects and burn away hostile vibrations.

2. The **RED SUN PLAQUE**

This creates the symbolic presence of Big Fire. The plaque has images of both the sun and the moon as well as the **White Hare** (symbol of the Moon Goddess) and the **Three-Legged Peacock** (symbol of the Sun God).

3. **KSIDDHIGARBHA with 3 CELESTIALS**

This powerful image is a stronger cure for subduing the *Three Killings*. This is excellent for households that suffer from regular abusive and angry confrontational situations. This remedy brings back some harmony to the family situation. It can also be an excellent way of suppressing hostility from outside forces.

STARS OF THE
24 MOUNTAINS 2013

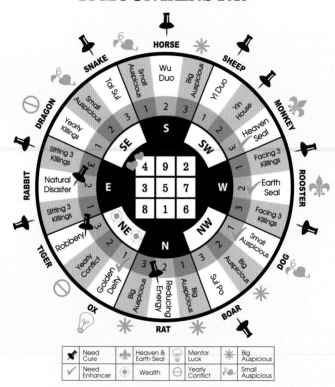

| ⚑ | Need Cure | ⚜ | Heaven & Earth Seal | 💡 | Mentor Luck | ✳ | Big Auspicious |
| ✓ | Need Enhancer | ◉ | Wealth | ⊖ | Yearly Conflict | 🐭 | Small Auspicious |

In 2013 we see a good number of auspicious stars, big as well as small and this is a very good indication of the year's outlook. The MONKEY enjoys the Heaven Seal Star but is flanked by the Yin House and Facing Three Killings this year.

INFLUENCE
OF THE 24 MOUNTAINS

To further investigate the luck of the year and the fortunes of the twelve animal signs, we look at the compass stars of the 24 mountains. These change every year, so their influence on the luck profile of the twelve animal signs also changes from year to year. Different lucky and unlucky fortune stars fly into each of the 24 compass sectors, bringing energies that either improve or decrease the energy of the twelve animal signs.

> The effect exerted by these directional stars is quite meaningful according to how they interact with readings of the other two charts. There are altogether 108 different fortune stars but only a handful fly into each of the 24 mountain directions in any given year.

These bring auspicious or harmful influences, but they vary in strength and type each year. The 24 Mountain stars that affect the twelve signs in 2013 are illustrated on the facing page. Note that the 12 signs occupy every alternate direction of the 24 directions around the compass. Inside each animal sign location is the mountain star on which the sign sits on.

When your animal sign sits on an auspicious star, it brings good fortune luck; and when it sits on a problematic star, it brings aggravations.

In 2013, the Monkey sits on the *Heavenly Seal* which brings support from heavenly deities. Place a symbol of Heaven near you or in the Southwest corner of your work desk.

PART TWO

LUCK OF THE MONKEY IN 2013

General Prospects for the Year

Wood Monkey – 69 years
Fire Monkey – 57 years
Earth Monkey – 45 years
Metal Monkey – 33 years
Water Monkey – 21 years

LUCK OF THE MONKEY IN 2013
Unexpected Success for the Monkey, without having to even try that hard!

The Monkey enjoys a very unexpected "bonus" year in 2013. This is the year ruled by its secret friend the Snake, a year when huge but unexpected SUCCESS comes your way without you having to do very much, a year when you might even be feeling weak and doubting your own abilities and despite this, something totally unforeseen happens which change your view of your future.

This year you will discover that you do not need to doubt yourself because something is happening in the cosmic realms to bring you something quite special. It will be different for different Monkey-born, but whatever the big surprise is, it will fill you with happiness and make you swell with pride. From this perspective, the *Star of Heavenly Seal* which has flown into your home direction becomes quite significant.

Your personal Wind Horse meanwhile is incredibly powerful in 2013 and this adds fuel to your success luck potential. The Wind Horse will ensure that the year turns out a lot better than you dream of, because it is the kind of good fortune happening that will take you into a NEW league altogether! The Year of the

Snake brings a bountiful goody to the Monkey due probably to your very special affinity with the Snake.

The Snake Year brings a calming and relaxing influence, which soothes the constantly active personality that you are, and this benefits you tremendously. The wisdom of the Snake Year's chi energies permeate into your consciousness and it is comforting because this year, the Monkey suffers from very low self esteem. This is mainly caused by the negative element profile affecting your inner essence, as well as your Life Force. Amongst the twelve signs of the Zodiac, it is the Monkey that suffers the lowest levels of chi energy in these two important categories.

As a result, you find it hard to motivate yourself. There seems to be a lack of vitality and vigour in the way you look at the world. This affects your relationships and your stamina gets lowered. It seems harder than usual to be active or to generate any kind of enthusiasm for anything at all. It is not a good feeling to have and it can be extremely distressing - and for some of you, it could even cause some level of despondency to permeate your moods.

At first, this feeling of negativity does not hit so hard. In February, when the year begins, you are still being supported by the energy of the previous Dragon Year, but as the year progresses, your energy levels will start to feel depleted.

This lethargy will go on well into the year and will only start to turn around towards the third quarter of the year. But by November you will start to feel more energized as this is a very auspicious month for you. It is likely this month when the help you are receiving from "heaven" manifests some amazing good fortune your way and it will be something that benefits you directly.

For the **69 year old Wood Monkey,** 2013 will continue to bring fantastic wealth luck your way, and this continues the good fortune you enjoyed in the previous year. Indeed for you there is both prosperity and success luck at its maximum so materially this should be a very good year for you.

In terms of Health luck it is the **33 year old Metal Monkey** who has the best of good health. This means that the illness star afflicting the Monkey's direction of Southwest will not hurt this Monkey as much. For other Monkey born, it is necessary to place the correct remedy to subdue the illness star in the Monkey's home location of Southwest 3. Especially for **57 year**

old Fire Monkey, whose health luck is weak and thus must watch this carefully. The Monkey also has to cope with an extremely low level showing in its Spirit Essence luck. Both this and your Life Force are at their weakest levels this year! These indications added to the presence of the illness star in the feng shui chart afflicting your home location suggests that you will definitely benefit from putting attention to strengthening your physical and mental wellbeing.

> The great thing about Chinese Astrology and Feng Shui is that these are practices that always have the correct remedies to overcome indicated afflictions. If you are familiar with these esoteric practices, it would not be difficult for you to subdue the specific type of negative energies indicated. Once put under control, the illness star affecting you will be less strong.

You can also use element therapy to improve your element profile for the year, thereby strengthening your weak Life Force and Inner Essence. Thus to improve vitality and energy levels, increase the dominance of Earth element in your living and work spaces. **Solid crystal balls** are excellent for this because they contain **condensed Earth element chi.** As for your inner essence, what you need is to increase the brightness in the rooms you occupy. Once you enhance your spaces this way, you will sense your positive feelings growing. The attainment of success and higher status will then come far more easily, as you will feel far better able to cope. Enhancing the inner essence makes the mind sharper and more focused, and confidence and self assurance increases. The great thing is that your energy and enthusiasm will likewise increase, and this makes for much better interactions with your loved ones.

Not everything will work out well for you immediately this year, as the feng shui winds can exhaust your energy levels BUT you will ultimately succeed in making the fullest use of opportunities coming to you. You enjoy excellent success luck & you have lost none of your intrinsic attraction.

The Monkey's aura may not be quite as dazzling as it can be, but you benefit enormously from the *Star of Heaven Seal* that seems to be bringing a slowly emerging self-assurance as the year progresses especially from your ally, the almighty **Dragon** whose luck is enormously strong and thus very beneficial. Also stay close to your other ally, the **Rat**, who likewise enjoys extremely auspicious luck in 2013. Both your allies enjoy quite outstandingly strong element profiles and the Rat benefits very much from very auspicious *Big Auspicious Stars*. So it benefits the Monkey to get really cozy with them during the Year of the Snake.

These two signs bring out the best in you, supporting you where you need it most and complementing your strong pointes in a very seamless way. They give a big boost to your inner confidence thereby helping you actualize your Success luck.

This will be your key to success – leaning on your allies and borrowing their cosmic strength to translate your efforts into manifest success. Work-wise you will then operate at a good level. In this Year of the Snake, the elements of the year that rule five important aspects of luck and vitality create your element profile for the year. This comes from the Monkey's Birth elements interacting with the year's elements. The indications of the five aspects of luck affecting the prospects for Monkey in 2013 are summarized in the table shown on the following spread.

2013	WOOD MONKEY 69/9 years	FIRE MONKEY 57 years
LIFE FORCE	Very Bad	Very Bad
HEALTH	Good	Very Bad
WEALTH	Excellent	Very Bad
SUCCESS WIND HORSE	Excellent	Excellent
SPIRIT ESSENCE	Very Bad	Very Bad

The indications of the five aspects of luck affecting the prospects for Monkeys in 2013 are summarized in the table shown here.

OF MONKEY 2013

EARTH MONKEY 45 years	METAL MONKEY 33 years	WATER MONKEY 21 years	ELEMENTS OF 2013
Very Bad	Very Bad	Very Bad	**FIRE**
Very Good	Excellent	Neutral	**WATER**
Very Good	Neutral	Good	**WATER**
Excellent	Excellent	Excellent	**WATER**
Very Bad	Very Bad	Very Bad	**WOOD**

This table in the previous pages have been laid out to give a super snapshot of how the elements of the year affect Monkey born people, categorized according to the heavenly stem element of their year of birth. At a glance, you can see that there is quite a heavy concentration of negative black pins in the first and last category of luck. But happily there is also equally excellent three stars indicated in the success luck category. The stars in the table here range from excellent to very good to good luck while the black pins suggest weakness, hindrances, aggravations and misfortune!

The three stars indicating excellent success luck benefits everyone born in the year of the Monkey with the **45 year old Earth Monkey** and the **69 year old Wood Monkey** enjoying the best wealth luck indication.

The Monkey is confronted with a very big drop in the strength of their Life Force and also Spirit Essence. These two categories determine how those born in the Monkey years react to events during the year, and how they cope with challenges and new opportunities coming into their lives. These luck categories also show how strong they will be physically and mentally. Here, the indications for the Monkey are that you will have a tendency to be weak…

What is being indicated is those born in Monkey years **will not** this year possess the toughness and resilience needed to respond with grace and strength to whatever the year brings; so you will need to be extra aware of this and think carefully before making decisions. You should also avoid being impulsive this year. At the same time, do not over commit in terms of tying up your time. Make sure to get enough rest!

Note that your LIFE FORCE refers to your level of vitality. Some years we are more vivacious and active than in other years, and this is always indicated by a good show of red stars in your Life Force. Vitality is said to reside in our hearts, and so it sustains our life. If this should be weak, it must be strengthened – as for the Monkey this year.

Your SPIRIT ESSENCE offers a window into the soul. Another way to express this category of luck is the luminosity of your spirit. Note that when the spirit is strong, it resides within the body, and when it is weak, it tends to wander outside the body, making you vulnerable to mischievous local spirits. This category of luck defines the quality of your inner chi, which has psychic connections to your outside environment. Thus the Monkey would be better off not to stay out too late at nights and not to be excessively foolhardy putting yourself at risk in whatever way at all. Remember that Monkey's Spirit Essence is at its lowest levels this year. This can cause you to be more vulnerable than ever to naughty wandering spirits. The local spirit landlords of your living and work spaces will also not be in sync with your inner energy. Your aura tends to attract hindrances from the spirits residing in the cosmic spaces around you, so it is a good idea to appease them with **spiritual feng shui incense offerings** on a regular or weekly basis. This will reduce small aggravating problems.

But the Monkey is enjoying maximum strength in your Success Luck. This year you have great success luck, a mega improvement over last year – cannot be better! This is why you can achieve quite a lot this year. The Success Luck indicator measures the power of your inner "Wind Horse" which carries the energies of your mind. The strength of your personal Wind Horse is the category of element luck which can be regarded as the most important. The good news is that for the Monkey-born, it shows three stars, which is the maximum! This means the Monkey's success potential this year is at its maximum. Your personal Wind Horse is at its highest strength. It is very meaningful when the Wind Horse is strong, because it can give a lift to the year as nothing else can. A strong Wind Horse has the power to lend strength to the other 4 categories of luck. When you enjoy a powerful Wind Horse, it means that those of you who have the ambition and determination to aim high will "fly like the wind horse in the sky" attaining whatever goals you set yourself.

To activate your personal Wind Horse, display a decorative **image of the Wind Horse** around you. The Wind Horse is usually shown as a precious white horse carrying a wish granting jewel on its back, a jewel surrounded by radiating rays of bright light.

The WIND HORSE is a powerful manifestation of your own auspicious mind and having an image of it near you brings exceptionally good spiritual feng shui. This is sure to strengthen your inner confidence in spite of your low level inner essence.

The power of the Wind Horse should never be underestimated – this is one of the great secrets kept hidden by the Astrological Masters and shared only with their favored disciples. In fact, references to the Wind Horse in Chinese texts are rare, and it is only in previously hidden texts on Tibetan Astrology that the secrets of the Wind Horse emerged during the latter half of the last century.

As for HEALTH LUCK, here it means the condition of one's physical body. In 2013, only the **57 year old Fire Monkey** manifests a serious weakness in health luck so for you strengthening the Wood element near you will help.

As for WEALTH LUCK, this refers to the stability of your finances during the year. When three stars are indicated, it suggests excellent wealth luck, indicating additional or new sources of income. This is enjoyed by the **69 year old Wood Monkey.** When two stars are indicated, as shown for the **45 year old Earth Monkey**, you will also experience good financial stability this year.

The Wealth Luck category is also an indication of your PERSONAL POWER, i.e. your ability to achieve the aspirations you set yourself. It refers to your moral strength and level of determination. When it is positive, as shown by the stars, it indicates that you attract prosperity and wealth using your own efforts, hard work and determination. When you activate your personal power, you will easily maneuver through obstacles and attract abundance.

When Wealth Luck is weak, as indicated for the **57 year old Fire Monkey** there is the possibility of financial disappointment or there can be delay in receiving payments due to you, or maybe your source of income dries up or you simply do not receive funds which you were counting on. This negativity can however be subdued by applying an element remedy. Here the feng shui solution is for the Fire Monkey to place Wood energy in the Southwest of your personal space as this will effectively "strengthen your own stem Fire element". This should help you stabilize your finances.

Benefitting from the Stars of the 24 Mountains

Monkey people also benefit from an excellent indication in the 24 Mountains compass stars of the coming Year of the Snake. This arises from the Monkey "sitting" on the *Star of Heaven Seal,* which is a very lucky indication. This star brings the approval, blessings and unseen hand of heavenly energy, which helps you in whatever you set out to do. The heavenly seal also brings invisible guardians who protect you from bad spirits who can cause misfortune luck.

According to astrological texts, different "stars" fly or migrate to the 24 different subsectors of the compass and these are known as the 24 Mountains. These "stars" have descriptive names and their influence on the animal signs around the compass can be positive or negative.

Feng Shui Masters of Hong Kong and Taiwan have great respect for the influence of these stars, and they always take account of the effect they have on the fortunes of the signs through the year. They also take account of these stars when doing the physical feng shui of houses and also consult the annual stars when analyzing the readings of luck prospects of different animal signs.

The effect of the 24 Mountain stars then, whether good and bad, is felt by the 12 animal signs because each of the signs' home location on the compass lies within the 24 Mountains. Every alternate 24 Mountains location is the home location of an animal sign. Sometimes the effect of the 24 Mountainz stars is so auspicious that they can cause windfalls to occur in the sectors blessed by the good stars.

Your luck prospects for the year are influenced by the 24 Mountains Star that your animal sign sits on. Your luck is likewise affected by the stars flanking your sign location.

The *Star of Heavenly Seal* is also useful in protecting the Monkey from the negative *Star of Yin House* on its right and from the *Star of Facing Three Killings* on its left. Both these stars are negative and do not bring good tidings. They should ideally be subdued, but this is not difficult to do, as you are already sitting on the powerful *Heaven Seal Star*.

Benefitting from the Feng Shui Chart

The Feng Shui Chart of 2013 is a very strong chart. This is because the chart is dominated by the number 5 in the center, making it in effect the **original Lo Shu magic square**. This is a phenomenon that happens every nine years, and when it happens, it strengthens the element energies of all the twelve animal signs. It also highlights the inner essence of the Lo Shu grid itself which is the basis of many powerful feng shui formulas.

2+8 =10   The most significant thing about the Lo Shu square is that the numbers facing each other on the compass eight directions add up to a *sum-of-ten*. Thus 2 of Southwest makes a sum of ten with the 8 of the Northeast and these two directions are directly opposite each other.

The sum-of-ten is an auspicious outcome in the analysis of relationships and also in their feng shui significance. This means that in 2013, all enemies have the potential to become luck bringing friends.

The Monkey and the Tiger can become good friends who can benefit each other in 2013.

Activating the Power of the Wind Horse

In 2013, your personal Wind Horse element is Wood, so a bell decorated with the Wind Horse flying into the skies with the Water element symbol at the base is extremely excellent as an activating symbol. Here the Water strengthens the Wood element of your Wind Horse and it is also the element associated with wealth. It is therefore very likely indeed that the Monkey has great wealth luck potential in 2013.

Displaying and hanging a single metal bell (can be brass) that has an auspicious image of the Wind Horse with the Victory Banner or a Wish Fulfilling Jewel on its saddle embellished on it is a very powerful way to cement your Success Luck.

The Monkey's personal Wind Horse is already very strong in 2013. Placing this activating bell in the Southwest sector of your home is to attract success to come all the time.

You can also position this bell in the Southwest corner of all your important rooms such as your living, dining or work room. You need only one bell, as too many will be excessive. Strike the bell each morning between 9 am to 11am the hour of the Snake to attract success. We recommend the hour of the Snake, because this is the year of the Snake.

As a item of jewellery, the Monkey will find it auspicious to wear a **Wind Horse Pendant** made of white gold and studded with some tiny jewels.

Anyone can invoke the power of the Wind Horse simply by hanging images of them as auspicious flags that are touched by the winds high above their homes. The Wind Horse has the powerful ability to completely destroy the unlucky influences of constellations and planets that may affect any of the animal signs in any given year. It has the power to make circumstances favorable. This is the main reason why Tibetans who believe strongly in the power of the Wind Horse have made hanging the Wind Horse as prayer flags surrounded by mantras such a cultural and popular tradition.

If you go to Tibet, and these days also Nepal, you can see colorful prayer flags fluttering in the wind, on roofs of houses, on temples, stupas and on all high places such as mountain passes. The Wind Horse prayer flags are believed to have the power to eliminate all bad and evil influences. What was originally an astrological remedy has taken on a spiritual dimension as powerful mantras and prayers have now been added to the Wind Horse images.

To invoke the power of the Wind Horse, display its image on a high place inside or outside your home – it can be as a figurine of a white horse with mantras or a pendant amulet or a **custom-made plaque** showing a white horse carrying special mantras and prayers of good omen. These are written on the plaque too, so that each time the breeze or the sun's rays touch the plaque, it generates positive and auspicious energy.

Displaying the Wind Horse image either as a figurine or as a plaque protects against hostile forces, and also assists you to enhance your inner vitality and good fortune. It also protects your home from being harmed by bad people such as those out to steal or hurt you e.g. burglars.

The Tibetans explain that bad people simply cannot enter your home, no matter how friendly they may be to your face, when your Wind Horse is strong or if its image is located inside your home.

Displaying the Wind Horse Plaque

The Wind Horse is always sketched as a white horse. It can placed in the center of a plaque or worn as a scarf. The horse has a flowing mane and tail, and on its back there is a **flaming wish granting jewel**. This is described as the gem that satisfies all desires. On each of the four corners of the plaque are the four protection animals that accompany the Wind Horse, the brown and black striped Tiger, the white Snow Lion, the Garuda, a mythical bird that control the air spirits and nagas of the underworld, and the Green Dragon. These four protector animals bring victory over the four fears.

Because the Monkey is blessed with such a powerful personal Wind Horse in 2013, invoking its power will ensure that whatever obstacles may block your good fortune will be easily eliminated.

MONKEY'S VITALITY & PERSONAL POWER NUMBERS

The table here reveals the Vitality and Personal Power numbers of men and women born in the year of the Monkey.

YEAR OF BIRTH/AGE	ELEMENT MONKEY	LO SHU BIRTH NUMBER	VITALITY NUMBER (in the SW of their magic square)	PERSONAL POWER # (in the NE of their magic square)
1944/69 YEARS	Wood Monkey	2	8	5
1956/57 YEARS	Fire Monkey	8	5	2
1968/45 YEARS	Earth Monkey	5	2	8
1980/33 YEARS	Metal Monkey	2	8	5
1992/21 YEARS	Water Monkey	8	5	2

The numbers 2, 8 or 5 interacts with the Vitality and Power numbers of the year 2013. When your personal Vitality number combines with the year's Vitality number to create the auspicious sum-of-ten, it suggests that the chi energy of the year brings you positive completion luck that suggests harmony, few obstacles and continuous good fortune.

When they are similar to the year's numbers, it means that the Vitality has been considerably strengthened. When the combination of the year and your own Personal Power numbers combine to create a sum-of-ten, your authority and status will show a noticeable improvement.

In 2013, the Feng Shui chart of the year indicates that the *Vitality Number* of the year is 2 and the *Power Number* of the year is 8. These numbers have a direct relationship with the vitality and power numbers of the Monkey.

From the table, check and see how your own Vitality and Power numbers interact with those of the year!

The Monkey's Ruling Trigrams

When investigating the feng shui and fortune of each of the twelve animal signs, it is useful to take account of the annual movement of the trigrams around the compass, which allocates a ruling trigram to each of the animal signs.

Your ruling Trigram exerts the greatest influence on your attitudes, tendencies and responses to events and people - both good and bad, both auspicious or which represent setbacks - that become part of your experiences.

When you know the general tendency you are born with as indicated by your ruling trigram, you will understand better how you will **react to the auspicious** developments of the year as well as to whatever setbacks may be in store for you. Every sign will see differences in their luck from month to month, and by knowing your ruling trigram, you will be in **better control of your responses**.

The table in the following page reveals the ruling trigram of all those born in the years of the Monkey based on year of birth as well as gender. The difference between men and women arise from the clockwise rotation for men and the anti-clockwise rotation for women.

YEAR OF BIRTH/AGE	ELEMENT MONKEY	RULLING TRIGRAM FOR MEN MONKEY	RULLING TRIGRAM FOR WOMEN MONKEY
1944/69 YEARS	Wood Monkey	Trigram KUN EARTH	Trigram SUN WIND
1956/57 YEARS	Fire Monkey	Trigram KEN MOUNTAIN	Trigram TUI LAKE
1968/45 YEARS	Earth Monkey	Trigram KUN EARTH	Trigram KAN WATER
1980/33 YEARS	Metal Monkey	Trigram KUN EARTH	Trigram SUN WIND
1992/21 YEARS	Water Monkey	Trigram KEN MOUNTAIN	Trigram TUI LAKE

69 year old WOOD MONKEY

MEN ruled by KUN the EARTH坤 – in 2013, you embody the nurturing power of matriarchal energy, even though you are in fact the Patriarch; you extend great warmth and caring energy to your family and offer unconditional support towards them. Good restful energy comes to you from the Northeast.

WOMEN ruled by SUN the WIND巽 – in 2013, you rule with an unseen hand. You are a gentle old lady indeed and are also generous to a fault, but let not anyone underestimate you. Even at your age, you will have great spirit, but you tire easily, so do take it easy.

57 year old FIRE MONKEY

MEN ruled by KEN the MOUNTAIN 艮 – in 2013, you are as unshakeable as the mountain; keeping perfectly still and very tranquil indeed. If you are a meditator, you are likely to be very good at it; perhaps even a Master and so there is great inner fortitude within you. But you are also a very down-to-earth and practical old patriarch, and you enjoy the respect of your whole family!

WOMEN ruled by TUI the LAKE 兑 – in 2013, you will be very alert to opportunities. You will also be sensitive to your surroundings and to new people coming into your life. You can be stiff and unbending too, and your most favourable chi energy will be coming to you from the West and Northwest. You will view anything coming from the South with great suspicion.

45 year old EARTH MONKEY

MEN ruled by KUN the EARTH 坤 – in 2013, you are practical and nurturing, and you in effect demonstrate the power of all-encompassing matriarchal energy that is part of this Trigram. You may in fact be the Patriarch of your situation, but your organizational and motivational skills reflect those of big mama! You will take charge of all you survey, but you will also show warmth and care to those dependent on you.

WOMEN ruled by KAN - WATER
坎 – in 2013 you tend to be even more mysterious than usual, and it should not surprise you that others will be a little afraid of you, and this is because you do tend to come across rather cold, deep and dark. Loosen up and you will have more fun!

33 year old METAL MONKEY

MEN ruled by KUN the EARTH坤 – in 2013, you show great potential to become the personification of the matriarchal energy that is embodied in this Trigram. You may be the Patriarch of your situation but you already demonstrate the practical abilities of the powerful organizer. This blends beautifully with your Monkey cleverness, and the more you yield, the more you win!

WOMEN ruled by SUN the WIND巽 – in 2013, you work hard and with great persistence to achieve your goals. You do well if you are in the media or communications industry. Your quiet determination will be your greatest strength this year, as will your industry and focus.

21 year old WATER MONKEY

MEN ruled by KEN the MOUNTAIN
艮 – in 2013, you are like mountain. Yours is a mind filled with ideas yet you are able to keep your thoughts to yourself. Like the mountain, you are able to stay perfectly still, keeping your own counsel and having an almost-perfect sense of timing. You are not a loud person despite being a Monkey sign, as you will raise your voice to be heard only when you have something truly helpful to say. Hence you build respect.

WOMEN ruled by TUI the LAKE
兑 – in 2013, you will be very alert to opportunities. You are sensitive to new people coming into your life and will tend to be more reserved than usual. Your natural instincts will make you less willing to trust the proclamations of would be suitors. Note that energy coming to you from the West and the Northwest are favourable, while anyone or anything coming from the South must be viewed with some suspicion.

PART THREE

ANALYSING YOUR LUCK IN EACH MONTH

Monkey's Powerful Wind Horse Benefits from Heaven Seal in 2013

While the Monkey's Flying Star and element luck indications do not look strong, you benefit from a powerful Wind Horse, indicating that success comes easily whatever may be happening in other areas of your life. So even if you may at times be filled with self doubt, you should push away feelings of negativity with the confidence that things work out well in the end. This year is also special in the sense that it is the Year of the Snake, your secret friend. It will thus be easy for you to seek out help when you need it; and just when you think you have exhausted all avenues, new ones open up; this is the meaning when you enjoy this kind of luck. You do have to be a bit more wary when fraternizing with certain animal signs this year, however; the Sheep in particular brings you quite negative energy. If you have someone close to you who is a Sheep, do carry the Horse amulet to dispel this compatibility affliction.

FIRST MONTH
February 4th - March 5th 2013

AN EXCEPTIONALLY EXCELLENT START TO THE NEW YEAR

The Monkey person should have no complaints with your luck this month! The wealth star has entered your chart, bringing with it also *Completion Luck*. This indicates that not only does everything you start meet with quite immediate success, you also have the ability to complete projects and bring things that may seem to have been dragging along to a successful close. If you stay focused, there is little that you cannot achieve this month. While you may be plagued by tired spells or bouts of exhaustion this year, if you pull yourself out of it by managing your eating, sleeping and health habits well, it should not be a problem for you. Enjoy the excellent stars in your chart this month, which you can enhance further by wearing the **infinity symbol**, or the **auspicious "8" in gold**.

WORK & CAREER - Applying New Skills

You can make big leaps and bounds in your career this month, catching the eye of decision makers who have the authority and inclination to fast track your climb up the career ladder. Be obvious about your contribution but try not to come across arrogant. There is no need to continuously brag and boast, but at the same time don't be overly self-deprecating either. You may be given the chance to apply a different skill in your work; this makes your job more multi-dimensional and a lot more interesting. Savour the opportunity and look on this as a platform from which you can leap onto the next level. You are likely to start seeing your career path open, giving you a whole new boost in confidence and morale.

BUSINESS - *Big Picture Approach*

There are many new opportunities presenting themselves, and there is no better time for you to move ahead strongly with expansion plans. Whichever decisions and directions you take are sure to go well if you are involved on a day-to-day basis. You have wealth and prosperity luck indicated, so do enhance the good energies of the coming month by consecrating **a new wealth vase** and placing it deep within your office. You may be made some offers that appear difficult to turn down, but consider your options carefully before you agree to anything. Be sure it is what you really want as something better could come along the very next day. Don't however let yourself be motivated by greed; looking for a bit more money here and there will cause you to make bad choices. Instead, look at the overall picture.

LOVE & RELATIONSHIPS - *Passionate*

A wonderful month lies ahead for the Monkey looking for love! There are many romantic interludes in store, but in your quest for love, beware of looking for the wrong things. Don't go for the obvious conquests that look good only on paper. Just because you can check off a few boxes does not make them ideal. Instead, follow your heart when you're searching for a soul mate. If you let your heart decide, it will not let you down.

> For those of you already married, you will find your spouse and yourself having lots to talk about this month. You are in a good mood, and this rubs off on those around you. You make your own reality and if passion is part of what you're seeking, boy are you going to have it!

EDUCATION - *Stay Focused*

A good time for self-improvement and for learning up new skills. The more focused you can stay, the better you will do. Don't be surprised however if you evoke some jealousy among your peers; when you do well, there will be those who are happy for you, and also those who will envy your success. This is a time when you get to see who your true friends are.

SECOND MONTH
March 6th - April 4th 2013

LUCK AFFECTED BY NEGATIVE WINDS; WATCH YOUR BACK

This is one of those months when a lot of bad could mask what is good. Overall you have underlying good fortune waiting to be tapped, but because of the negative winds blowing your way, it can become difficult to see the opportunities amidst the setbacks. Obstacles crop up more often than usual, and this can put a huge dampener on your spirits. The *number 7 robbery star* also makes it difficult for you to trust others, and even friends can appear to let you down. You do however have the *Ho Tu combination* on your side, which brings auspicious outcomes. Brush aside small misfortunes and don't let minor aggravations get you down. If you remain optimistic, there is a lot to be gained this month.

WORK & CAREER - *Keep Your Spirits Up*

Although work may be tough going, keep your spirits up. A dreary attitude could put you in a downward spiral and lower the opinions others have of you. Things may not go as planned and you may have a mishap or two. If you make a mistake, take steps to correct it rather than look for excuses or for someone else to blame. Trying to cover your tracks will only make you come across incompetent and deceitful. But an instant reaction to remedy your mistake will be viewed favourably indeed. Maintain the pace you've been working at or you could find yourself losing steam just at the point when you need to power on ahead. Do not trust others easily. Be prepared to help others, but if you have crafty colleagues, you will need to be as crafty as them to stay ahead. This month is peppered with potholes for those who are not careful. Watch your step, and your back.

BUSINESS - *Beware Troublemakers*

There may be disputes when it comes to money matters between business partners. But before you jump to any conclusions, make sure you have investigated thoroughly before making accusations. Don't fall for third party troublemakers trying to come in between you. But do watch your back because you could be in danger of being let down by those you trust. Go with your own judgement when it comes to making decisions. Although you may be used to consulting with others before proceeding, your own decisions will probably be the best ones this month, not just for yourself but for everyone involved. Because you are exposed to the robbery and loss star this month, avoid investments involving large capital outlays and keep a close watch on finances. Avoid unnnecesary risk-taking.

LOVE & RELATIONSHIPS - *Emotional*

You may come under stress which could lead to some emotional outbursts, causing confusion and strain in your relationships. If you make it a habit to communicate more with your partner, you are less likely to crack under the pressure. Learn to relax because there are many happy moments to be had. Don't let your dismal mood drag your spirits down, because this will only make you ineffective in your work, which could then lead to a full-blown downward spiral. Be thankful for life's little pleasures and you will be surprised how a happy disposition can make everything go better for you. Use the power of your mind to overcome any negative feelings, and your relationships will start to go much better.

PERSONAL SAFETY - *Be Careful*

Be more vigilant when it comes to personal safety. Bad things only need to happen once. Avoid staying out too late, don't walk in alleyways, check that the security features in your home are working, and remember you can never be too careful. It is also a good idea to carry the **White Elephant Amulet keychain** against loss and robbery.

THIRD MONTH
April 5th - May 5th 2013

BACK ON TRACK - INVOKE YOUR HEAVENLY SEAL!

This month goes much better for you, with many new opportunities opening up. You enjoy luck from heaven, which makes things proceed smoothly and without incident. Helpful people enter your life, and when you need someone in a certain position or with a specific skill to help you, you are sure to find them. You can further activate your good fortune luck this month by carrying the **Heavenly Seal amulet**. This will ensure you are able to make the most of your good fortune luck, and that golden opportunities do not slip through your fingers. For the younger Monkeys, when advice is given to you by older folk, do not dismiss them. Listen to suggestions that come your way; and count yourself lucky to be able to benefit from this kind of advice.

WORK & CAREER - *New Ideas*

All your undertakings go well. Even those you thought unlikely to succeed will turn out better than expected. The energies of the month make this a good time to propose or develop new ideas and new initiatives. Your colleagues and other associates you encounter in your job respond well to you, and it is easy for you to become close to others. You work well in team situations; in fact you thrive. Your popularity makes you a good candidate for team leader and puts you in a good position for the next round of promotions. You are at the peak of your powers and should not waste this month lying low. Use this time to apply yourself fully and to make real progress onwards in your career path.

BUSINESS - *Cool Negotiator*

You are feeling confident and composed, which puts you at ease in most situations. You are a cool negotiator and can talk just about anyone into your way of thinking. This makes this an ideal time to enter into new deals and to negotiate new terms (should you need to) with those you do business with. You hold the trump cards, but also possess incredible charm, which makes others feel like they are gaining just as much as you from whatever you are proposing. You have the knack of pitching everything just right; those of you bidding for contracts and concessions have a very good chance of being successful this month.

LOVE & RELATIONSHIPS - *Many Admirers*

Your enthusiasm and optimism attracts all kinds of admirers, and when it comes to love and romance, you will have no shortage of suitors this month. Although you are picky, you are also too nice to let others down too directly, so you could well find yourself going on several dates a week, with a different partner each time! While there is nothing wrong with having plenty of friends, but just be careful that friendships do not blur into romance, especially when there are more than just the two of you involved. The Monkey sign has the ability to invoke great jealousy amongst their admirers, and you don't want to find yourself trapped in the middle of some kind of love triangle. For those of you already in steady relationships, this is a fabulous month to tie the knot, or to become more serious with one another.

EDUCATION - *Good Advice*

The younger Monkey enjoys mentor luck this month, and if there is an older person willing to fill that role for you, make the most of it! If you need advice, you don't need to wait for it to be given; ask for it! Don't try to make big decisions on your own. While ultimately whatever you choose will be your own decision, input from others who have your best interests at heart can only benefit you.

FOURTH MONTH
May 6th - June 5th 2013

BE VERY MINDFUL OF WHAT YOU EAT AND DO NOT OVER STRESS

The Five Yellow pays a visit, making life more difficult. This malevolent Earth Star joins the number 2, another troublesome Earth Star, to bring misfortune, especially in the form of illness and accidents. Do not put yourself in danger. Watch what you eat as there is risk of food poisoning, which could be severe. If you are a participant in high-risk sports, be more careful or even abstain for the month. Don't drive too fast, don't be careless, and wear or carry **protective amulets**. Misfortune can also arise in the form of aggravations in daily life, which could cause you mental distress. When met with problems, remember to *think* before making your next move. Being impulsive is probably the worst thing you can do right now. Lie low, let the situation pass, and devise a well-thought-out strategy before doing anything.

WORK & CAREER - Avoid Conflict

This is not a good month on any front, and you are likely to be in a bad mood because of it. Don't try to fight off your mood. Instead, it is easier to just avoid potential conflicts by withdrawing. Trying to resolve matters by some kind of compromise will only end up making things worse. Just accept that you are not the easiest person to work with this month, so try not to subject others to your disagreeable disposition. Even if you are in need of support, watch you do not over lean on others, or they could start to despise it, especially if you are taking the credit for their work. Things are still political, so watch how you act and what you do if you don't want to become a target of office politicking.

BUSINESS - *Hold Steady*

Avoid acting impulsively. With the energies as they are, be prepared for the worst to happen, and expect to encounter problems and obstacles on a regular basis. The good news however is that your problems will not be insurmountable; you will be able to overcome them and find workable solutions. Do not let apparent blocks to your success upset you too much. Even when deals are nearly through and last minute glitches cause it to fall through, try to imagine that there must be a reason. If you go with the flow, things will pick up again next month. Right now you may not be able to see who your supporters are, but this will all become clear enough soon enough. Use this time to extricate yourself from partnerships and associations that have stopped working.

LOVE & ROMANCE - *Differences*

There is danger of many differences in opinion in your relationships. Those of you who are married could get into some incredible conflicts, only because you know in the end you will forgive one another. If your relationship is not so firmed up, conflicts to escalate to a point where it is simply easier to walk away. If you are with someone who means a lot to you, you may have to make a real effort if you want to make it work. Don't let moments of anger or frustration cause you to spoil something that has a lot of long term potential. Watch your words; they may be offensive enough to be irreparable. You have a real knack of saying the wrong thing this month, and sometimes you could find yourself doing it nearly on purpose, just to get a reaction. But remember, with the energies as they are, the tipping point is closer than you think. Avoid attention-seeking in this way or you could cause some damage that could take a long time to put right again.

HEALTH - *Poorly*

The combination of the misfortune and illness star is a venomous mix when it comes to health issues for the Monkey. For those of you who are already suffering poor health, take extra care this month. Don't expose yourself to too much stress or this could become truly hazardous to your health.

FIFTH MONTH
June 6th - July 6th 2013

FEELING WEAK AND SUCCUMBING TO TEMPTATION

You get along so well with others this month that it may start to scare you. Even the people you usually avoid become interesting to you, and you find yourself able to make conversation about anything and everything. Those of you in what you think are unfulfilling marriages or partnerships could become vulnerable this month to advances from outsiders. Watch you don't allow infidelities, no matter how small, to ruin things for you. You're suffering from weak morale even as you appear strong and confident to outsiders, and this makes for you to be taken advantage of, especially when it comes to romantic interludes. For those of you in established relationships, flings are the worst idea and should be avoided at all cost. This is however a promising month for young Monkeys pursuing their studies or just starting out in their careers.

WORK & CAREER - Good Ideas, But Distracted
You are feeling creative and those of you able to apply it to your work have a good chance of making great advances in their careers this month. You have many

good ideas and the good news is that they are likely to meet with positive response when shared. But you need to watch out for the *Peach Blossom* influence on your life right now. Some of you may find activities in your personal life affecting your ability to concentrate at work, while others of you could well meet romantic temptation at the workplace. Either is bad, so work at putting better focus on your job if you want to keep up a good impression with the boss.

BUSINESS - *Network Aggressively*

Your strength this month is in getting along with others. You have a real ability to crack jokes at just the right time, and you gauge your audience well. This makes this a good time to strike up new deals, to impress those you need to impress, and to network aggressively. You possess the talent to pitch new ideas and to give convincing and deal-closing presentations. Those of you whose work involve research will also make some exciting break-throughs this month. Where you need to be careful however is getting romantically involved with the wrong person. Beware illicit trysts; these will come back to haunt you no matter how innocent or unplanned they may have been. Even if you are single, a romance with the wrong person could cause great scandal to erupt, and a wrong spin can be put on even the most innocent of motives.

LOVE & RELATIONSHIPS - *Be Careful*

While Monkey people will not be lacking opportunities when it comes to romance, there is real danger of your getting involved with the wrong person. Those of you who are married need to be particularly careful that you do not succumb to temptation and put everything you have at risk. Work on your relationship with your spouse. Make time to spend together if your work has been keeping you apart. You may be feeling lonely or in need of company, but you will find just as much solace in the arms of your spouse as in the arms of someone else. And with your spouse there will be no messy aftermath to deal with. Wear the Double Happiness pendant to protect your marriage from predatory outsiders, and carry the Anti-Infidelity Amulet to keep you safe from temptation.

EDUCATION - *Scholastic Luck*

The young Monkey benefits incredibly from the influences of the *Scholastic Star* this month! As long as you do not let romance cloud your focus, you have the potential to do very well in your studies. Those taking exams can expect good results if you have put in the work. Activate study luck with a **Crystal Globe** placed in the Southwest.

OM AH RA PA CHA NA DHI

SIXTH MONTH
July 7th - Aug 7th 2013

QUARRELS AND MISUNDERSTANDINGS GET YOU DOWN

This month will not be an easy one for Monkeys. The quarrelsome star causes strain in your relationships, both business and personal. Try not to take anyone for granted. Watch your conduct with unknown quantities, and make every first impression count. You have to work harder at getting along with people, and if you lose your patience, it is probably due to your own quarrelsome energy. Be more tolerant of others if you want them to like you as well as respect you. Your success is dependent on getting good support from others, but if you keep falling out with your allies, you could find help from here drying up. But don't put too much pressure on yourself, and avoid anyone who makes you feel bad about yourself.

WORK & CAREER - Watch Your Back
Constant conflicts of opinions make life at work particularly aggravating this month. You are constantly being misunderstood, and communication with others becomes tense, making things sometimes very unpleasant. You find yourself having to watch your back

because you feel unsure about who is really on your side. While there is no need to get overly suspicious about the motives of others, it is a good idea to watch your step and to play your cards close to your chest. Don't be too eager to share your opinions. This is also not the time to meet up with people where making a good impression counts. It is a better time for quiet research-type work than for giving presentations or pitching deals or proposals.

BUSINESS - *Conflict Situations*

Making money could be high on your list of priorities but wealth luck will only materialize for you if you put in a lot of hard work and effort. The main problem for you is the quarrelsome energy that seems to follow you around. You find yourself in conflict situations even with those you ordinarily get along well with. Others do not seem to be falling for your natural charm the way they usually do. You are very upfront with your words, and this could prove disastrous under certain circumstances.

While exciting new opportunities may present themselves, be careful how you negotiate deals, or things could go sour when a misunderstanding arises. Avoid entering into new partnerships this month. When it comes to signing agreements, it is also wise to postpone till next month when your luck improves. There is also risk of getting entangled in lawsuits and court cases. Those of you facing problems of a legal nature will need the **Flaming Magic Wheel with Sword** to counter the negative energies this month. You can also carry the **Double Ring Magic Fire Wheel amulet**, which will subdue quarrelsome energy directed towards you.

LOVE & RELATIONSHIPS - *Be More Tolerant*

Relationships may be stressful this month due to your argumentative nature. Don't let small things spoil things for you with friends or lovers. You are stressed out enough as it is in your work, and do not need something else to worry about. If you make it a point to be more tolerant, and to take an interest in what other people are doing or thinking, you will find all your relationships much more pleasant. You will also be more popular with others this way. Try to be nicer. Don't snap or lose your temper; doing so will be detrimental to your health, but worse, to your relationship, so of which may never recover from one too many outbursts.

EDUCATION - *Mishaps with Friends*

Mishaps with friends could get you down, affecting your ability to concentrate when it comes to your studies. Put less focus on your social life and more on your work, and you will find you will be much happier this way.

SEVENTH MONTH
Aug 8th - Sept 7th 2013

DANGER OF BAD ILLNESS...
SO BE EVER MINDFUL

The illness and accidents star gets doubled, making it really quite dangerous for the elderly Monkeys among you. You are also more at risk if you are already weak, or you happen to be living in a Southwest room of the house. Misfortune of this kind can come from falling sick or from meeting with avoidable accidents, and either could put you out of action for a while. It is vitally important therefore to nullify the double black star by carrying the **health amulet.** You can also wear a **Wu Lou in gold**; this will also promote better health as well as counter the malevolent Earth energies of the stars in your chart this month.

WORK & CAREER - Work With Others

You may want to take a backseat at work this month. If you have been focusing too much energy on one thing, you could find yourself start to meet with diminishing returns. Don't try to take on too much, and work with others when you can. Put differences you have had with colleagues and co-workers aside. This is a good time to eat humble pie and admit if you need some help. Use this time to build on camaraderie with those you work with. This will improve and increase what you can achieve, and it will also make you feel a whole load better. Even if you have good ideas, don't try to show up your colleagues because you need them more than they need you. Be prepared to share credit for work done; it may even be a good idea to let someone else enjoy the recognition. This is not your time to shine, but you can benefit in other ways.

BUSINESS - *Be Meticulous*
Wealth luck is down and you could find it more difficult to close deals and make money. Sales may be slower than usual. Even if you are usually the sort with infinite ideas, this month you may find it difficult to be creative and original. Don't hope to hatch mind-blowing ideas. Instead, focus on getting the job done. Be meticulous in checking details or you could make some costly mistakes. Keep a watch on expenses. Your cash flow may not be so healthy. Do not overexpose yourself and do not spend unnecessarily.

If your cash flow is tight, display **a pair of camels** in the office to help protect the business.

Be careful when embarking on new projects. Avoid pursuing radical, untried strategies for now. Even if you think you have spotted a golden opportunity, it is better to wait till next month before moving ahead.

LOVE & RELATIONSHIPS - *Support System*
While luck is down elsewhere, those of you with supportive partners will find them a tremendous source of support this month. Be open with each other. If you are facing problems at work, share them. Holding back will only drive a wedge between the two of you. Being secretive is worst of all; this could lead to jumping to conclusions that could be harmful to your relationship. For those of you who are single, it is probably not the best of times to pursue new relationships. You are not at your best and whoever you are out to impress may get the wrong impression of you. Wait until next month when it comes to trying to take things to the next level in new romances and relationships.

EDUCATION - *Under the Weather*
The young Monkey pursuing their studies could find things getting more tricky this month. You are not as sharp intellectually, mainly due to your feeling under the weather. Get enough rest and don't try to work too hard. There are times when putting in the hours gets you results, but this is not one of those times.

EIGHTH MONTH
Sept 8th - Oct 7th 2013

FEELING COMPETITIVE
AS YOU REGAIN PHYSICAL STRENGTH

The *Victory Star* enters your chart making you feel strong again and imbuing a competitive streak in you. Any problems that stumped you before seem quite manageable now. You start to achieve things more effortlessly because you don't put too much energy into why something will not work; instead you look for alternative solutions if the obvious ones prove too difficult. You can expect some significant turning points this month, and although some of them will jolt you out of your comfort zone at first, you will soon start to welcome the change. Once you have adjusted to new circumstances you find yourself in, you will start wondering why you hadn't discovered them before. This month is a journey of learning, and some of the things you discover will prove quite magical indeed.

WORK & CAREER - *Go Beyond Your Job*

This is a busy month for you at work, and the good thing is you will have the energy to back it up. You are feeling much stronger again, and you are also in much better spirits, which makes you a magnet for other positive people. Use this time to get your ideas into play. Your opinions are valued, so make an effort to share them. The more involved you get with the others you work with, the more valuable a team member you will become. This is also a good time to work towards any promotion you are hoping for. Go beyond your job if you have to. Even if it means putting in extra hours, extra time, or entertaining out of work, your dedication to your job and your boss will not go unnoticed.

BUSINESS - *Effective Delegation*

A great month for Monkeys in business! You have a convincing air of authority, which makes you an effective boss and leader, so use this time to motivate those who work for you and to galvanize the team. The better you can all work together, the more effective you can be as a group. Don't try to do everything as a one-man-show. Effective delegation, as long as backed up by true leadership, will be more rewarding and successful than trying to get things done all by yourself. This is a good time to think of expansion and of increasing sales and profit levels. You have the luck to spearhead new initiatives, so if you have good ideas in the pipeline, you can feel confident about putting them in motion now. Nip any petty politicking in the bud. If there are scuffles amongst your staff, put a stop to it. It is not necessarily a good idea to hope for them to sort it out amongst themselves. If there is something you can do, get involved. You have the magic touch when it comes to appeasing others this month.

LOVE & RELATIONSHIPS - *Fulfilling*

Matters of the heart go well for you, bringing you satisfaction and personal fulfillment. Your positive attitude and cheerful disposition rubs off on those around you, so your relationships with others will tend to go very well. Make time to look inwards and focus on the family. If you have been feeling guilty about neglecting them a little, you can more than make up for it now. The single Monkey hoping to find love could get lucky this month! This is a time of new beginnings, and for some of you, it may indicate the end of one relationship and the beginning of another. Don't cling on to something that is no longer working. Don't be afraid to let go, because oftentimes, what lies ahead is so much better than what you leave behind.

FENG SHUI ACTIVATOR: The best way for you to activate the *Victory Star* this month is to carry the Victory Banner and to display one in your personal sector of Southwest.

NINTH MONTH
Oct 8th - Nov 6th 2013

GETTING BACK ON TRACK AS MENTAL AWARENESS IMPROVES

You start taking a bigger picture approach to your work and life in general, and this allows you to enjoy what really matters most. While you may meet up with obstacles along the way, this new clarity of thought lets you understand that sometimes what may at first appear to be disappointments are actually blessings. When you change your attitude, you find yourself happier, more effective and more successful. The results of this change in mindset are almost immediate; so when things don't seem to be going your way, take a pause, and start looking at things a different way.

WORK & CAREER - *Mellow Down*

You are raring to go, and this may make others appear half-asleep and dawdling. Don't let your impatience rub others up the wrong way, because while you may be feeling stronger, you still need their help. Stop yourself when you find yourself about to snap at someone. Others will not appreciate your curtness, so mellow down and take a different approach. Be crafty and wily, and use your natural wit and charm to get your way in negotiations. Don't brandish your authority around or you will find yourself making enemies that you don't need. It may an idea to limit your contact with others when you are feeling irritable, because when that side of you surfaces, you could have a big falling out with what would have been a useful ally. Beware workplace politics.

FENG SHUI ACTIVATOR:
Keep a **Rooster** on your work desk to peck away at gossip and scandalous chitchat. The Rooster sign also forms the *House of Commerce* with the **Monkey**, so having a Rooster on your desk will also bring you luck in your career and in business.

BUSINESS - *Long-Term Luck*

Things may not always be smooth this month, and there will be many challenges to face. Those of you in competitive industries could see more challengers entering the fray. While immediate prosperity luck may be elusive, you do enjoy long-term wealth luck, so use this month to lay down plans for the future. Don't expect to make quick money; your luck does not indicate instant money. What it does point to however is success in the future that looks to be sustainable and long-term.

LOVE & RELATIONSHIPS - *Fast-Paced*

You won't be short of passion in your life right now. Things tend to be fast-paced for you in all aspects of your life, and when it comes to love and romance, it is no different. There are many exciting moments in store, but if you are looking to find someone you can be with into the long-term, you need to be more discerning in your choice. Make you decisions based on your circumstances, but don't go breaking too many hearts, or in the end it will be you who ends up getting hurt. For those married or attached, you'll see your relationship improve. You will become even closer, and the conversations you share become real conversations about things that really matter. Your love mate could well turn into your soul mate this month.

EDUCATION - *Master Something*

While you may have a lot of energy this month, it may not be such a good idea to take on too many different things. It is better to focus on a few things and on doing them well. Continue to work conscientiously. If you find you have too much to cope with, try turning to others for help. Don't insist on getting everything done yourself.

TENTH MONTH
Nov 7th - Dec 6th 2013

A VERY EXCELLENT MONTH WHEN GOOD THINGS MATERIALISE

What an awesome month for the Monkey! You enjoy good fortune luck in your career and also in your personal life. There are small and large pleasures to enjoy, and your highs come as much from everyday delights such as spending time with the family and kids, as it does from success at work and in business. Make the most of this time when the wealth star combines with the number 2 star to form the auspicious sum-of-ten. The stars point to the completion of projects and to successful endings; so things you have been working on may finally produce meaningful results. There is fulfillment both of the financial and psychic kind. You have the winds of fortune blowing on you, so do not let any negativity enter your mind to cloud your judgement.

WORK & CAREER - Turning Point

This month could prove a real turning point in your career. You are rich with new ideas that could revolutionize the way you do your work. Impressing bosses becomes your specialty this month. Remember that ideas will stay ideas unless you put them into practice. When implementing a new idea, remember also that without hard work and follow-through, even the best-laid plans could fall by the wayside. You could meet up with obstacles, but your willingness to overcome them will be enough to ensure success in the end.

BUSINESS - *Good Opportunities*

Whatever directions you choose to go in pursuit of will tend to do well this month. You enjoy the wealth star, and combined with the number 2, it indicates successful completion of whatever ventures and projects you get involved in. There is great wealth luck indicated and this can be strengthened by wearing **wealth symbols** as jewellery, and by consecrating **a new wealth vase.** Place your new wealth vase deep within your office once you have made it, and if you make it with the right motivation, its positive effects will be even greater. Some very good opportunities come your way. Make time to consider them; sometimes even when something appears far-fetched, it could work. And who knows? It could work beyond your wildest dreams!

LOVE & RELATIONSHIPS - *Uplifting*

This is an uplifting month for those in relationships. There is good news just around the corner. If you have been waiting for something to happen, this could be the month that it finally does. It doesn't matter who is the dominant one in the relationship, but if you are ready to take things to the next level, and your partner has made no indication, pipe up with what's on your mind! Your partner may have been waiting for you to give some indication. If you are going to last as a couple, don't be shy or coy about these things. Talk marriage, engagement, living together… even the commitment-phobic among you will start to enjoy the idea of finally settling down.

FENG SHUI ENHANCER: Wear the **8 Auspicious Objects pendant in 18K gold** to activate the power of 8 and the auspicious completion energies in your chart this month. The 8 Auspicious Objects bring complete good fortune and attracts both material as well as spiritual luck.

ELEVENTH MONTH
Dec 7th 2013 - Jan 5th 2014

GOOD LUCK STILL, BUT GUARD AGAINST BEING TOO TRUSTING

You have the *Robbery Star* in your chart again, causing money loss and betrayals. This month it is better to tread carefully and beware who you trust. Go with your instincts but try to have the whole picture before making any decisions. Don't be overly impulsive with anything. Your cash flow may be strained with all the unexpected expenses cropping up, so don't go overboard with the spending. Watch the violent number 7 by carrying the **Nightspot Amulet**; this will help protect against snatch thieves and petty criminals. You should also carry the **White Elephant Amulet charm**. But despite the unfortunate 7 in your chart, it does combine with the 2 to form a lucky *Ho Tu* mix, bringing good fortune luck. So problems will tend to solve themselves, and all things work out very well in the end.

WORK & CAREER - *Don't Make Mistakes*

Be careful at work; there could be enemies in the ranks waiting to stab you in the back for their own gain. Try not to trust anyone. Even those who consider themselves your friend may betray you for their own gain, and the worst thing is they may not even see it as a betrayal! In their mind, they could well find a line of thought that seemingly "justifies" their actions. Your best defence is not to open yourself up to that kind of risk. Be extra careful about not making mistakes. If you do have a blunder, don't try to hide it. Own up to it but start taking immediate steps to rectify it.

BUSINESS - *Maintain Status Quo*

Avoid exposing yourself to anything too different this month as the energies are not in sync. It is easy to make mistakes in areas you are unfamiliar with, so when there are doubts over how good your luck is at any point in time, it is better to maintain the status quo. Don't venture outside of your comfort zone, because the punches you take could set you back a few steps. You are at risk of being cheated, so be more careful on this front. Competitive pressures heat up, so there is no time to relax, even when you feel mentally drained. Work closely with your team so you do not have to shoulder all the responsibilities single-handedly.

LOVE & RELATIONSHIPS - *Beware Scandal*

Those of you in steady relationships will find their partners extremely supportive this month. Sometimes your partner may offer an opinion you don't immediately agree with, but take what is said seriously as there may be some valid points there. Romance is there but it may not be scorching; rather it is gently simmering under the surface and you will find yourself in love like a married couple rather than a couple of newly-weds. If you are looking for more passion, it is up to you to spice things up.

For those of you still single or "on the prowl", there is no harm in having some fun on dates, but avoid fooling around too much, or a scandal could break out, causing some harm to your reputation, with repercussions affecting your job, family life and social status.

EDUCATION - *Set Your Own Standards*

Try not to compare yourself too much to others. Judge your own successes by how much you have improved, rather than by how well you are doing compared to your peers. In the end, good exam results come about from conscientious and hard work. Over comparing will just get you feeling down or inadequate... not the best ingredients for a top student!

TWELFTH MONTH
Jan 6th - Feb 3rd 2014

HEAVEN & MENTOR LUCK BRING UNEXPECTED HELP

The Year of the Snake comes to a successful close for the Monkey, with the *Heavenly Star* paying a visit. You have unseen cosmic forces helping you along, causing you to make all the right choices. Go with the flow and let your instincts guide you. If something does not feel right, don't try to make it right. Change direction instead. This is a time when everything really does happen for a reason. The cosmic forces are at work showing you the way. You also enjoy terrific *Mentor Luck* this month. If you already have an obvious mentor figure in your life, pay more attention to what he or she has to say this month. You have plenty to learn from those older or wiser than you. If you cannot think of a mentor figure you look up to currently, perhaps just such a person will turn up in your life very soon. Keep a watch out.

WORK & CAREER - Trying New Things

This is a good time to get moving in your career. There are people in the right places to help you, so it is worthwhile to put in the effort. Life at work is highly satisfying and could find you getting involved in all kinds of activities, causing the scope of your job to expand somewhat, much to your liking. How much you benefit from the new opportunities coming your way depends on you. There is a high chance for a promotion of some kind if you indicate you are willing to take on more responsibilities. Be courageous about trying your hand at new things. Even if you are asked to work on something you are unfamiliar with, view it as a chance to try something new. Who knows what hidden talents you can unearth? You get along well with everyone, which makes things so much more pleasant.

BUSINESS - *Be Patient*

When it comes to business matters, the advice is the same… go with the flow. Deal with sudden changes in circumstances by being adaptable. There is no right or wrong way to do anything. You will pick a different choice depending on what day of the week it is. But this month you can trust that whatever it is you choose, you will make the right choices, or ones that are at least right for you for the moment. Once you have chosen to go down a path, don't then backtrack before you even have time to sample the outcomes of your choice. Give everything time. Look on your choices as seeds that need to germinate and grow. Success may not come right at once, but it will come if you stay true to yourself and maintain your optimism and your confidence.

LOVE & RELATIONSHIPS - *Friendships*

There's a lot of love in your heart and it comes from a feeling of security. Surround yourself with people who love you the way you want to be loved. Don't hang on to relationships that make you question yourself. Life is too short to waste on those who do not appreciate you. This month may be more about friendship than romance. You find you have as much time for your buddies as for your love interest. And if you are having a hard time when it comes to dating and relationships, your friends are going to be your best bet to haul you through difficult times. If you are in a steady relationship, don't fret over unimportant differences in opinion. Learn to let go. You don't need to win every argument to feel good. In fact, when you feel OK about losing is when you have won.

EDUCATION - *Exciting Times*

There are many exciting developments for the young Monkey. Embrace them with open arms. If there is something new you want to pursue, be open to discussing your thoughts with someone older that can advise you. You enjoy quite wonderful *Mentor Luck* this month and you stand to benefit from the wisdom and judgement of just such a figure, only because they can provide an alternative and more worldly viewpoint. Ultimately, your choices are your own, but when made with their input as well, your choices can be spot-on.

PART FOUR

YOUR RELATIONSHIP LUCK IN 2013

Benefitting from Mentor Luck this year

Everyone of you born in the Year of the Monkey possesses a natural charisma, an adorable sense of fun and a cheekiness which few can resist; so for most of you, getting along with others is quite a breeze. Mainly because you do enjoy the company of others – being basically a very sociable animal – ready to party at a moment's notice...

COMPATIBILITY
With Each Animal Sign

COMPATIBILITY	LUCK OUTLOOK IN 2013
MONKEY with RAT	Complementing each other magnificently
MONKEY with DRAGON	Astrological allies helping each other
MONKEY with SNAKE	A very happy year for these "secret friends"
MONKEY with MONKEY	A neither here nor there relationship
MONKEY with TIGER	Might work but both harbour suspicious vibes
MONKEY with OX	A truly excellent relationship
MONKEY with RABBIT	A difficult time for you to work things out
MONKEY with HORSE	Can benefit but might not be on same track
MONKEY with SHEEP	Nothing good can come out of this pairing
MONKEY with ROOSTER	A great year for this partnership!
MONKEY with DOG	Attraction here sparks creativity & a happy outcome
MONKEY with BOAR	Boar 's charisma wins over the Monkey

... but Monkey people tend to get their love lives all muddled up because you are the type who wants to be friends with everyone. The Monkey is spontaneously charming, but as you get on in age, you will find yourself feeling less and less comfortable in the company of too big a crowd.

In the Year of the Snake, despite this being your secret friend, you unfortunately seem to be quite lacking in energy. Your usual radiance shines less bright, and you no longer enjoy being the life of the party. Your friends see a more down-to-earth Monkey, who is also less ready to trust and definitely less eager to take risks.

In the coming Year of the Snake, the center of the Feng Shui chart is dominated by the ultra strong misfortune star 5, and so one would be forgiven for jumping to the conclusion that the hostile energies of past years would likewise prevail this coming year. Happily, this is not the case. The Snake Year reflects the calm and almost intellectual thinking nature of the astrological Sign of the Snake.

The influence of the Snake's demeanour encourages deeper thinking and there is a tendency towards good analysis preceding impulsive actions in all interpersonal situations. In past years, anger energy dominated the world's environment, which culminated in the excitement of the Dragon year when many of the world's countries saw significant changes in leadership and/or major transformations of focus.

With the quieter, less noisy Snake sliding into the world's consciousness, many start to feel an air of calm that reflects the Snake's influence. 2013 also has a Year Pillar which shows that *Water is subduing Fire*. As a result, there is a calmer, more reasoned approach prevailing; people will generally be more patient and tolerant, even when this might go against their nature.

In other words, this is a year when the **head rules the heart**; when patience wins over impulsiveness. Emotional outbursts will be reduced and so will the violent energy that caused so many arguments and misunderstandings to rise to the fore previously.

As a result, the coming year will see a lot less anger and a lot more goodwill in relationships. There is less hostility and fewer angry words, which reflect the Snake year's Naga energy. In 2013, we live through a year of the Water Snake, and this creature signifies energy of a more docile nature. All this has an effect on the Monkey's personality. You too exhibit a calmer, more quiet and serious face.

Nevertheless, do take note that it is still a NAGA year, and nagas can be quietly deadly when and if provoked. It is thus advisable to be wary of sudden and hidden stings in relationships. The less anger-ridden environment notwithstanding, we must also note that human nature is not 100% tolerant. There will always be anger reactions that can boil over. Remember also that suppressed anger can often be more dangerous than explosive anger.

> Thus while it is a benign Snake with no venom that rules the year, it is not a pushover scenario. The Snake Year will see the presence of goodwill energy, but there is also a hidden hardness. We cannot forget that the number 5 i.e. the deadly and potentially hostile wu wang is in the center of the chart.

Here, it is extremely vital to keep the energy emissions of the Five Yellow, the *wu wang*, totally subdued in the center of the chart. Subduing it effectively requires us to use a more powerful remedy than the **five element pagoda** cure which we have been using in the past few years, although this continues to be a good cure, especially when they are new and have not become exhausted from having absorbed too much of the negative chi energy of 5 through overuse.

For this year, with the Five Yellow dominating the center of the chart, all homes should strive to maintain good feng shui and also to create good harmony in the home and office. To ensure this, there are **three powerful remedies**:

1. First is the placement of the five-coloured strongly decorated **Kalachakra Stupa** with powerful Kalachakra mantras filled within. This remedy will subdue the powerful impact of the Five Yellow.

2. Second is the use of the **7-level pagoda** which will not only keep all afflictive quarrelsome energies locked inside the pagoda, but will also be a powerful deterrent against all nagas, so that stay benevolent throughout the year. Those of you familiar with the legend of the White Snake who

went into battle with the monk will remember that the White Snake was finally subdued with a 7-level pagoda. Note that what we are aiming to do here is merely to *subdue* and not to vanquish the naga.

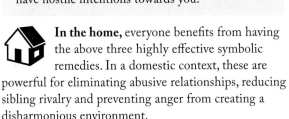

3. Third is to place the high potency **Three Harmony Warriors Mirror** with the three symbols of victory in the fight against disharmony. These three symbols are the **8 legged lion**, the **fur bearing fish** and the **sea conch dragon**. This well-guarded secret is found in lineage texts from Tibet and its used by ancient masters to subdue enermy forces who have hostile intentions towards you.

In the home, everyone benefits from having the above three highly effective symbolic remedies. In a domestic context, these are powerful for eliminating abusive relationships, reducing sibling rivalry and preventing anger from creating a disharmonious environment.

In the office, these symbols, especially the third remedy, are excellent for reducing office rivalry, subduing petty politicking and promoting teamwork and cooperation amongst office staff. The **mirror effect** absorbs all that is negative in the environment and dispels them into the cosmic abyss.

Note that all three cures have sacred syllables and words that empower and activate them. With these cures placed in the center of the home OR the center of the living room (on a coffee table or sideboard) the positive traits of the original Lo Shu square with the 5 in the center can then flow freely through the living or work space.

It also encourages the special feng shui relationships to manifest more easily and here we are referring to the very auspicious *sum-of-ten phenomenon* which gets created by the original Lo Shu. This arrangement transforms every sign's astrological enemy into a potential friend.

2+8 =10 **The Monkey's astrological enemy is the Tiger.** This year, the feng shui chart numbers are 2 for the Monkey and 8 for the Tiger, generating the *sum-of-ten phenomenon*. This creates not only goodwill between the two signs but also brings good fortune when the two signs collaborate or come together as a team or couple.

In 2013 therefore, interactions between Monkey and Tiger create the potential to be mutually beneficial, forming a partnership that leads to gains and good fortune. Whatever hostility vibes between them that manifest are more likely to dissipate, even though astrologically they are usually considered to be enemies. They will be friends in this Year of the Snake!

The effect of the sum-of-ten extends to your relationships with other signs. Note however that the Monkey is not feeling very sociable this year, mainly because your Vitality is at a low level. There is a high likelihood that you are feeling lethargic. There could also be self image issues that whittle at your confidence. You are not so fun to hang out with this year, but despite this, you are still as likeable and as popular as ever.

The chi energy of the year brings out all that is weary and suspicious in the inner subconscious world of the Monkey. You will continue to be as warm and as tolerant to those close to you - your family, lovers, spouse, children - but you will be a lot less trusting of "outsiders", especially those you work with i.e. colleagues, employees, bosses and business associates. To the latter, you will be more wary and suspicious of motives. You will have little time for those who annoy you. As a result, your relationship vibrations will depend on who you are interacting with. Nevertheless, all the latent charm for which the Monkey born is well known for will continue to be evident, and friends do not desert you. But this is not a year that is conducive to making "new" friends.

> There are also occasional misunderstandings, especially with those born in the year of the **Rabbit**, the **Boar** and perhaps others born of your own sign of the **Monkey**. But whatever differences that might surface should blow over quite quickly.

The Monkey will find that you are usually the weakest one in your interactions with others. This reflects your unconscious feelings of insecurity. You are in a weak place mentally, caused by your weak inner essence, so for you, simply being nice could take an effort. Indeed, you are reluctant to be sociable, and this is definitely not a year when you are prepared to go out of your way to be helpful to others.

Other years, the Monkey is a lot more helpful and warm, but with your confidence levels this year at a lower level, your focus outwards tends to be a lot less positive. This is a temporary condition and we all go through periods like this. For some of you, this will be more pronounced than for others, but your great success luck this year should strengthen your confidence levels.

Remember when you feel low, that it is "all in the mind". Make an effort to get out of this negative syndrome and you could achieve a lot more this year, both in terms of getting material success as well as in winning friends and influencing people.

In 2013, the Monkey person MUST make a very special effort to get out of the "negative syndrome" caused by its low level of inner essence luck. Think of your strong Wind Horse and let this enhance your confidence to actualize your fabulous success luck potential.

It benefits the Monkey to positively turn on the charm, to make the effort to be extra warm and accommodating to those you work or do business with, even though you may feel reluctant or disinclined to do so!

The Monkey's Allies

Your allies are the Dragon and the Rat. Together, these three signs create the *Trinity of Zodiac Competitors*. When these three signs get together, they can infuse one another with a zest to beat all others in whatever endeavours they are engaged in. In 2013, the Monkey is the weakest of the three, and as such you MUST take strength from your two powerfully strong allies.

HOROSCOPE ALLIES		
RAT, DRAGON, MONKEY		
OX, SNAKE, ROOSTER		
TIGER, HORSE, DOG		
RABBIT, SHEEP, BOAR		

As a group, you have a very competitive attitude that differentiates you three from the other groupings. But this might well get diluted by your general feelings of inadequacy, and also the affliction of the illness star - these feelings can dilute the strength of this trinity.

For the Monkey, your Achilles Heel this year will be your feelings of lethargy. Motivate yourself strongly and shake off all the feelings of weakness and you could well surprise yourself with how effective you can be.

The good news is that in 2013, the Monkey gets along extremely well with the Dragon, with whom you could get romantically involved. The Dragon is brimming over with confidence. Thus springs attraction between the two of you. Animal signs generally interact in a positive way toward their Zodiac allies, and the Dragon is the Monkey's ally.

To enhance your relationship, make sure you create good relationship feng shui in your surroundings! The extent of affinity magnifies or gets reduced according to the quality of the feng shui energy around you. It is also helpful to investigate the level of affinity you have with your allies in different years. In 2013, the Monkey is compatible with the Dragon, but there could be minor aggravating problems in this relationship emanating from the Dragon's mood swings and the Monkey being illness-prone.

Meanwhile, the Monkey also has the potential of creating a magnificent relationship with the Rat. Thus from both allies, the Monkey stands to gain quite a great deal of strength and luck improvements. But it helps very much when the environment is also energized with feel-good chi. This means placing all the CURES needed to subdue the feng shui afflictions of the year.

It also means dispelling all negative energies by keeping the "spirits" of the land happy with regular offerings of incense, especially "white incense" i.e. incense made from the resin or fibre of trees with white barks. These are referred to as white incense which includes sandalwood and frankincense. Incense ensures that spiritual feng shui is well taken care of by keeping the local landlords of your home happy and contented.

The Monkey and its allies are known for their determination to succeed in the face of competitive pressures; these are dynamic people, strongly self-motivated and highly-disciplined. You generally work well alone or as a team. But it is important for there to be mutual admiration between you and whoever you work with. Respect is something the Monkey, Rat and Dragon do not give easily – whoever interacts with them must earn their respect.

All three tend to have a high opinion of themselves, irrespective of how they may be feeling subconsciously, so there is a certain amount of dogmatism to their views. The Monkey is very individualistic as are the Dragon and the Rat, so relationships between these allies can be "argumentative", but underlying their arguments will be genuine respect for each other.

The Rat, Dragon and Monkey form the
Astrological Trinity of Competitiors.

MONKEY WITH RAT
Complementing each other magnificently

The Monkey feels drawn to the Rat and this turns out to be a mutually beneficial relationship in 2013. The main problem here is the Monkey's low Vitality level this year, lacking the energy and inner confidence to keep up with the Rat, yet NOT lacking in Success Luck! So it really is up to the confident Rat to lend you, its great friend, some of its own inner and physical strength.

The good news is that this is a really good year for the Rat to be doing this. The Rat finds your sense of humour and witty brain attractive, so there are plenty of good love vibrations flowing between the two of you. Also, the Monkey makes the Rat feel a surge of power energy, simply because you, the Monkey, needs and wants the Rat's attention and focus. This alone will create the energy for you both to achieve a great level of affinity.

So if meeting for the first time, you the Monkey could cause the Rat to get all gaga so that you can both barely contain your amorous feelings. The **sizzle of attraction is instant and electric**. With those you have already forged a relationship with, the affinity between you continues to be strong, and the dependency factor causes both to be even more enamoured. For the male Monkey, this quality of attraction is mesmerising, and for the female Monkey, the tendency is to feel very close towards the Rat lover. What is very encouraging for this pair is that the luck elements of the two of you indicate that Rat's Water element brings big success luck to the Monkey, so from this perspective, this is a very good year for the Monkey who pairs up with the Rat.

> However, the Monkey is blessed with the *Heavenly Seal* this year and this enables Monkey's charisma to radiate wonderful rays of cosmic heavenly chi to assist the Rat in all its endeavours. This pairing thus has the potential to be quite magnificent in terms of the happiness it can generate for these two signs.

The problem in this relationship is that the Monkey is not an easy person to catch, and even those already in a committed relationship with the Monkey will find that staying faithful is not something that comes easily to the Monkey.

Happily for the Rat, in 2013, the Monkey tends to be more home bound and will gravitate towards the strength and display of self assuredness exuding from the Rat. So here the Rat will exert good influence, keeping the Monkey grounded, less flighty and definitely more interested and committed. This is definitely a pairing that is worth pursuing.

MONKEY WITH DRAGON
In 2013,
astrological allies helping each other

The Monkey and Dragon are like two peas in a pod. They belong to the same affinity group and thus have a great deal in common. They are both equally driven in their quest to succeed and to win in whatever situation they find themselves in. To triumph over the competition, you two are really prepared to sacrifice everything for the greater good – which is to win! Except that in 2013, the Monkey will find it harder than usual to keep up with the Dragon who is brimming with confidence and moving at the speed of light!

Happily for the two of you, the year 2013 finds you both perfectly complementary for each other in terms of the success luck category you both enjoy, which is at maximum level. Except that here it will have to be the powerful Dragon who must take the lead, as this mighty sign is both physically and spiritually stronger than the Monkey.

There is thus enough Dragon energy to fuel the superlative success energy, which both of you have! Your personal charts indicate that you are both blessed with powerful Wind Horses, what we refer to as your "*Lung Ta*", which does not allow anything to stand in the way of your achieving all that you set out to achieve". What the both of you must be clear on however is that in 2013, the Monkey must rely on the Dragon to supplement its Life Force and Inner Essence, and this means relying on the Dragon for support, determination and confidence levels. But this is easy as you are two signs that complement each other, so this is a happy pairing with a good future.

Your energies can intertwine like heaven and earth reflected in your elements of Earth and Metal, and also in the stars that fly into your base locations on the compass – the Dragon has the *Small Auspicious Star* next to it, while the Monkey sits on the *Heavenly Seal* suggesting that there is unexpected and hidden assistance flowing from the cosmic heavens.

For those of you in a dating relationship, the year brings love and the promise of marriage. In fact, this is a good year for you both to tie the knot, even though it is a year missing the *lap chun*. The Dragon's mighty energy can overcome this! For those already in a committed relationship, your bond will move steadily and grow from strength to strength. This is a year when helping each other bears delicious fruits – a rich harvest indeed!

MONKEY WITH SNAKE
A very happy year for these "secret friends"

The Monkey's relationship with its Secret Friend, the Snake, is closer than ever. These two signs are always good for each other, even when you come from different social backgrounds.

In 2013, the usually noisy and jumpy Monkey, who will be a lot more subdued this year, is very drawn to the quiet demeanour of the Snake.

Neither of you are strong this year. Life Force and Inner Essence of both causes there to be a general lack of vitality, and even a shortage of self confidence. But instinctively, you gravitate towards each other, and you give one another an inner strength that makes you very comfortable with each other. This is a very sweet pairing this year.

In 2013, yours will be a calm and restful courtship, with neither wanting excitement or needing much from each other. The feng shui winds bring a restful, loving energy to the Snake, and this proves attractive to the sign of the Monkey who has to contend with the illness star of 2. The Snake is the Monkey's secret friend, and in

2013, it dominates the year, but it takes tremendous joy in the Monkey's charismatic glow, which comes from you sitting on the *Star of Heavenly Seal* in your compass location. The cosmic energy of the Monkey thus brings special magic into the relationship with the Snake.

But the Monkey is flanked by afflictive stars brought by the 24 Mountains Compass and may tend to be difficult at times. It is important for the Snake to overlook the occasional outbursts of impatience from the Monkey and be aware that being difficult and even stubborn are strong Monkey traits. As long as both can tolerate each other and also embrace a slower pace, the year will bring a restful happiness.

In 2013, the Monkey and Snake both enjoy being free of major expectations placed on themselves. This year, you are both happy to be contented human beings, and you will reject anything that puts pressure on you. Not for you both the hectic pace of mad achievement.

The Monkey and Snake are Secret Friends and are extremely good for each other.

You are happy to let the year take its course, with you sliding easily and happily into a slower, gentler pace. The Monkey, to a very large extent, feels this way, as you are slowed down by the energy winds of the year. The Snake feels the same way, so the two of you are a good match. Nevertheless, don't think there are no unexpected goodies in store for you!

This is because despite not trying too hard, the Monkey experiences big success luck, which comes from your strong personal Wind Horse. For the Snake too, there is a series of small Successes all through the year. These lift you both aloft. It is the best kind of feeling and makes 2013 a year filled with many satisfying joyous moments for the both of you.

SECRET FRIENDS		
RAT and OX		
BOAR and TIGER		
DOG and RABBIT		
ROOSTER and DRAGON		
MONKEY and SNAKE		
SHEEP and HORSE		

MONKEY WITH MONKEY
A very neither-here-nor-there relationship

This year, the Monkey's relationship with its own sign is fraught with ambivalence and lethargy. This is the effect of you both coming under the influence of your weak element profile for both your Life Force and your Inner Essence, which causes you to feel dispirited and not very motivated at all.

Instead of the usual vivaciousness you are both capable of, you suffer from the "cannot be bothered" syndrome in 2013. So there is really nothing very much that can come from a union of two Monkey signs!

It is a neither-here-nor-there relationship, so if you are meeting for the first time, this makes both disinclined to take the friendship to a deeper level; and should you already be in a committed relationship, there is danger that you could simply tire of each other, completely immune to whatever glow you may emanate for others. You simply cannot see very much in each other, especially if you are in a love relationship. Those in a work partnership however might be more inclined to work on one another's success potential, and here there could well be sparks in the coming together of two Monkeys. Here you will both feel the hidden power of the Wind Horse within you. This comes from your own powerful minds, which can get stimulated by the *Star Of Heavenly Seal*; and when this happens, as when you focus your mental efforts on some project, it could take you aloft and jumpstart your energy levels.

This requires the both of you to create a scenario that is conducive to igniting the energy that lies latent within you.

First, you should strongly subdue the *illness star* affliction that causes the both of you to feel a lack of energy.

Secondly, make efforts to surround yourself with plenty of **Earth** element chi (with **solid crystal balls**) to enhance your Life Force.

Third, make your personal spaces **bright with stronger lighting** to increase the strength of your inner essence.

These steps will help the two of you – individually, as well as working as a team – to get motivated. And then the pairing of two Monkeys will be a magnificent success, bringing a joyousness that is sorely lacking in the Monkey's horizons this year.

The **crystal balls** create powerful concentrated Earth chi and we have designed some amazingly powerful crystal balls embellished with secret mantras that enhance the crystals even more.

These are thus excellent for enhancing the Monkey's Life Force. Then shine a row of lights (use light-emitting diodes) directly at the crystal and your inner essence gets increased! These are secret feng shui cures that manipulate the chi energies around you using element therapy remedies.

Crystal balls of the 5 colours represent all the elements harmonizing to bring auspicious good fortune. Crystals also enhance your Life Force which is very low this year.

The Monkey's Astrological Enemy

Usually, when two animal signs confront one another, as in the case of the Monkey and the Tiger, one being Metal, the other being Wood, and one being Southwest while the other is at the other end, the Northeast - all kinds of difficulties arise in any relationship that cause them to come together.

This is part of the astrological forces that create animosity and ultimately mistrust. Most years, this relationship can lead to various obstacles and problems that reflect and manifest their latent hostility. Animosity is worse when the two are in a sibling relationship.

But once every nine years, the cosmic forces that influence relationships can cause zodiac adversaries to be more than cordial – in fact, can cause these same adversaries to be extremely beneficial for one another.

The transformed energies come about as a result of the re-emergence of the original Lo Shu square, which causes the numbers of the square to arrange themselves in a way such that all signs confronting each other at opposite ends of the axis will have numbers that add up to ten – this is the extremely lucky *sum-of-ten phenomenon.*

MONKEY WITH TIGER
Might work
but both harbour suspicious vibes

The Monkey in 2013 can get along with its opposing sign the Tiger, and in fact might even derive benefit from this "astrological enemy". Here we see two impetuous yang individuals, who generally have little in common and would under normal circumstances not be good for each other, becoming quite unlikely partners in the Year of the Snake.

These two signs can be quite strongly and irresistibly drawn towards each other from the start of any meeting and in 2013, they can indulge their mutual attraction all they want. This is because 2013 is the year when they will bring good fortune to each other.

Theirs will be a relationship full of laughter and high adventure. There is intensity and extreme energy generated between the two of you, simply because the adventurous streak in the Tiger will stimulate the Monkey out of its lethargy. The Monkey is galvanized into action as this is a pairing that generates great passion indeed. There will be drama and high emotion involved, and we can even describe this as the ultimate love-hate relationship. Continually matching wits and challenging each other, they will view life as a special game of one-upmanship between them both, with neither one prepared to give in to the other.

Both signs are poor losers, and there is nothing graceful or diplomatic in the way they act out their anger or love towards each other. Both Tiger and Monkey can be highly strung when riled, and they are definitely incredibly individualistic. All of which makes for a high level of passion that can tire out the Monkey!

It is important both signs recognize that this is not a year to stretch their respective emotions too far. Both Monkey and Tiger may be good together and Tiger's luck is excellent, benefiting as it does from the auspicious 8, but note that in terms of their element profiles, neither Tiger nor Monkey have very strong Life Force. In fact, Monkey's Life Force is at a very low level and Monkey is also afflicted by the illness affliction, so physically, the Monkey can be vulnerable.

ASTROLOGICAL *Enemies*

Besides the underlying *sum-of-ten* nevertheless, do remember that Tiger is still the Monkey's astrological adversary. So there is a lot of push and pull going on here. Both signs are determined and impulsive people. If their relationship works, it will be because they understand their own extrovert natures as well as their respective vulnerabilities.

But because they are NOT naturally compatible, remember there is always the possibility that this is a relationship that can experience a dramatic break-up in the longer term. Their magnificent fights will easily exhaust them, to the point of breakdown.

A Monkey/Tiger match can end up being one long, angry, simmering bonding, and if the relationship does go sour, the break-up is sure to be unfriendly. Note here that the Tiger's natural element is Wood. The Monkey's natural element is Metal.

In the cycle, Metal destroys Wood, as a result of which it will be the Monkey who dominates the relationship, and who eventually takes the upper hand. Here alas, the Tiger's ferocity will be no match for the Monkey's ingenuity. In 2013 however, it is the Tiger who is the stronger of the two!

MONKEY WITH OX
In 2013, a truly excellent relationship

In 2013, the dynamics of the Monkey/Ox relationship is complicated and not immediately easy to unravel or understand. This is because the two of you have very divergent luck in 2013. You are also two very different types of people with very opposite personalities. BUT if the two of you do get together or are thrown into each other's ambit, you will find yourselves unrelentingly and irrevocably drawn to each other.

The Monkey is especially drawn to the Ox as you see in this solid sign a strength you instinctively feel that you lack this year. Quite rightly here, your instincts, spurred on by the *Star of Heavenly Seal*, is steering you in the right direction. Hence the irresistible attraction.

Happily for the both of you in 2013, the passion between you gets fired up and continues to burn for quite some time. This will be a truly excellent relationship that brings plenty of urgent desperate happiness for you. It will appear hard to understand how the solid, staid and conventional Ox could even be remotely attracted to the unconventional, extravagant and flamboyant Monkey. Yet if you two meet under the right circumstances, you do and will get caught up in each other. One sees the other as refreshingly different, and becomes the perfect foil for the other. Here is potentially a delightful match indeed. And helping you along are the chi energies of the year as well as the feng shui winds that create for you both a very beneficial scenario.

To start with, the Ox enjoys the power of 8 which brings wonderful relationship luck – and the 8 that flies to the home location of the Ox forms a *sum-of-ten phenomenon* with the 2 of the Monkey. These are auspicious indications and they fan the energy levels of both signs, although in this relationship, it will be the Ox who leads and who calls the shots. The Monkey is more than happy to go along so that together they make brilliant, beautiful music together.

If you are in a love relationship, the two of you will be besotted with each other, with the Ox especially enchanted by the Monkey's ingenuity. The Ox will find that in 2013, he/she will follow the audacious Monkey who brings a fresh impetus to the Ox's endeavours. There is promise of much happiness indeed.

As long as the attraction between you can last, you are sure to benefit each other. The only problem is that Monkey's inner essence is low in 2013 and because of this, very much depends on the Ox keeping the vigour in this relationship going.

> What the Ox should know is that the presence of the Monkey near the Ox brings out all that is excellent in the Snake Year! Why? Because the Monkey is the Snake's secret friend, and it has the symbolic key **to unlock all the goodies of the Snake Year.**

Hence despite your low inner essence, which is directly causing the Monkey to feel less confident this year, you are in reality enjoying some great and hidden advantages over all the other twelve signs.

The Monkey and Ox can make beautiful music together, jiving to the beat of the Snake year!

MONKEY WITH RABBIT
In 2013, a difficult time for you to work things out

In this relationship, neither the Monkey nor the Rabbit derive anything special from the other. It is a very *blah* relationship and both will find that the year does not look after either of you very well.

The winds are blowing against both of you, and the Rabbit can be a big hindrance to the Monkey. In 2013, both will feel that it is a difficult time, and it is a year which hinders rather than helps their relationship.

These two signs can mesmerize each other with their quick wit and their wicked humour. Both signs are clever and can be funny individuals, sharing artistic and intellectual pursuits. At their best, they make great platonic friends. In that kind of relationship, enjoying one another is surely effortless. And for all kinds of reasons, they really should not go beyond these superficial boundaries. Because should they get serious with each other, they will simply waste away whatever goodwill they may have generated, and romance simply causes friendship vibrations to fly out the window. On almost all kinds of living issues, you are two people who cannot be further apart. Ideologically, you really find it hard to agree on anything.

So no matter how much fun you may find in each other, 2013 is simply not a good year for you both to work through a relationship. Whatever you do together becomes a tough decision, even when it is something simple like choosing which restaurant to eat in and which movie to see. You can see then that things just get petty. While other couples can simply laugh off their different tastes and inclinations, the two of you could start a war on simple things like that.

> At first, the Monkey and Rabbit find each other's company refreshingly enjoyable, but when the two of you start getting close, that is when the differences emerge.

In 2013, the Monkey will not have its usual enthusiasm and vitality to fall back on – and the lethargy just makes this pairing difficult. There is definitely a **mismatch of chi energy**, so better not to pursue this relationship too far. Better to postpone serious decisions to the following year. Furthermore, the year looks like it is filled with challenges for you both – as a couple and also individually. There are differences in your attitudes and many unimportant issues tend to get magnified.

The Rabbit will be the first to take flight, as this sign very rightly deems the relationship with you simply not worth pursuing, preferring to work through the year's lack of incentives alone.

Plus the Rabbit's natural element is Wood, while that of the Monkey is Metal. In the cycle, Metal destroys Wood. Thus the relationship will see the Monkey being too hard for the fragile Rabbit to endure. Any marriage between these two signs this year could well become a very unhappy pairing indeed. Better to postpone till the following year! Your respective element profiles are not at all good for each other.

The Monkey and Rabbit can stay friends if their relationship is an arm's length one. But get closer, and cracks start to form.

MONKEY WITH HORSE
In 2013, can benefit, but might not be on same track

The Monkey and Horse can have a good relationship, but are unlikely to inspire very deep feelings with one another. You are not a pair who can sit and chat about philosophy into the early hours of the morning, being both doers rather than thinkers. But you come into your own if you go seeking adventure together. That is when the inner core of your beings become strongly motivated and positively challenged. On this basis, you can get really close.

The year 2013 brings only averagely good fortune for you as a couple, and should you develop a love relationship, you will at first discover that your energetic, restless and amiable personalities match beautifully. There is excitement and a joyous feeling of comradeship. Both of you are blessed with naturally friendly natures, so on the face of it, yours seem potentially able to develop into a deep and long-term happy relationship.

The Monkey and Horse are two signs who will take the trouble to be nice to each other, rarely taking offence, seldom getting into disagreements over petty small issues, and always willing to see just the good side of each other. So the two of you can benefit from one another, and any union between you can be productive and successful. It is possible that you can accomplish significant things together, as both will keep your wilder more temperamental side in check.

In 2013 however, both the Horse and Monkey lack the impetus to take any kind of initiatives with one another. This reflects the somewhat introspective moods that might take hold of the both of you.

Also, 2013 is a year when both of you suffer from low self confidence, and there seems to be an inability to get things moving. You are not the action-oriented personalities of recent past years.

Your respective Life Forces are also weak, although this does not prevent the Monkey from benefiting quite substantially from heaven's help! The Monkey sign enjoys the *Star of the Heavenly Seal* and its element profile for the year indicates a strong and powerful Wind Horse. This brings success luck, adding an invisible cloak of attractiveness to its aura. So the Horse is certain to find its Monkey friend very appealing indeed. The good news is that feelings of attraction

between this pair are likely to be reciprocated. You are
also sure to be very supportive of each other.

Both Monkey and Horse are independent and clever
personalities, so there is an absence of clinging
behaviour, something both of you find very unattractive
indeed. You will enjoy and take pride in one another's
strengths and capabilities, and both of you will be
equally happy having independent careers or building a
business together.

> There is much that one can teach the other and
> the alliance will benefit from shared intimacies and
> ambitions. **You work well as a team because your
> talents are complementary**, the Horse being a solid
> worker (when he buckles down to work) and the
> Monkey being shrewd and very resourceful.

The challenge of 2013 is to overcome your weak energy
levels. Here, using your strong minds to push yourselves
into action is the key to success. Only then can the two
of you find real focus and then ride on the same track.
Otherwise each of you will go your own separate ways!

MONKEY WITH SHEEP
In 2013, nothing good can come out of this pairing

The Monkey and Sheep are not on the same wavelength in 2013 and their element profiles are so at opposite ends of the spectrum that instead of coming together, they will naturally have an aversion for one another. So these two signs are not at all good for one another in 2013. Their personalities will simply be at odds with each other.

This lack of goodwill between you in 2013 is caused by the stars of the 24 Mountains Compass, which brings the *Yin House Star* to sit between the two of you in the Southwest. As a result, you each cause yin spirit formation to the other.

This year, the charts suggest that you are far better staying apart, and those meeting one another for the first time should really not even give yourselves a chance to fall for each other. Better to wait until another time when the energies between you are more in sync.

AMULET CURE: If you are already married, the Sheep would benefit by having the **image of the Snake**, as this acts as an amulet, causing whatever harmful vibes that are brought by your partner to dissolve. Here, we are using the cosmic power of the nagas to eliminate the yin spirit formation caused by the pairing of you two signs. The Monkey should carry the **Horse amulet**.

These are special amulets which can be placed inside a small container and worn or carried. Another way is to place them inside images of the Snake or Horse and place inside the home. (Please email **amulets@wofs.com** to get these amulets.)

If you are in a business partnership and not a marriage, you can place the same remedial cures in the office and things should work out well. But do note that while the Sheep has strong Life Force and Inner Essence, its success luck is just the opposite - it is weak.

The Monkey on the other hand has excellent luck with a very powerful Wind Horse that brings success, but its Life Force and Inner Essence are weak.

Those in a business relationship should thus leave it to the Monkey to call the shots and make all the strategic-type decisions. The Monkey's luck and judgement will pan out better. In short, you, the ingenious Monkey, must be in charge.

> The Sheep's natural element is Earth. That of the Monkey is Metal. In the cycle, Earth produces Metal. This indicates that while the Monkey is the natural hands-on leader in this relationship, it will be the Sheep who must provide sustenance and support.

In 2013, the Monkey enjoys cosmic assistance from unexpected sources brought by the *Star of Heavenly Seal*, so the Monkey can indirectly benefit the Sheep. But there may be obstacles that prevent even this indirect benefit, so those of you already in a relationship should make sure you carry the **astrological amulets** so that hindrances afflicting this relationship are properly subdued.

MONKEY WITH ROOSTER
In 2013, wow what a great year for this partnership!

The Monkey and Rooster have a great deal of commercial compatibility, and in 2013, the coming together of these two signs taps into the presence of BOTH the *Heaven* and *Earth Seal Stars*. The Monkey sits on the *Star of Heavenly Seal*, while the Rooster sits on the *Star of the Earth Seal*.

This pairing of heaven and earth is incredibly auspicious as the relationship then embodies the sacred trinity of heaven, earth and mankind; what in feng shui is referred to as the trinity of the *tien ti ren*. This means that in 2013, the both of you can start any business together and it will have great potential for success.

The Monkey and Rooster together tap into excellent Heaven and Earth energy in 2013.

EARTH

In a love relationship, it signifies a coming together of two powerful forces that can sustain a long term relationship that is auspicious and fruitful.

In 2013, the energies of the two of you are complementary, but with the Rooster being stronger physically and spiritually and Monkey with a much stronger personal Wind Horse. But Rooster's Wind Horse is also strong, so together as a pair, you can soar powerfully into the skies, giving yourselves free rein to your joint ambitions.

Neither of you will hesitate about getting into a relationship, even though you both have startlingly different personalities. But you do have similar goals and aspirations. Both of you enjoy the fine things in life, and pursuing prosperity comes naturally to the both of you. It is in the way you attain your aspirations that might differ. The Monkey is a lot craftier, being excellent at the "art of war" in business, while the Rooster tends to go by the book and can be naive.

As such, the Monkey, though weak, can achieve more than the Rooster, as the Monkey will usually be familiar with all the short cuts!

But because in 2013 you bring luck to each other, the sum of both your parts is definitely more effective than either of you on your own. In a love relationship, it is the same, because you will both have similar priorities. Creating a good life is always paramount in your mind, so this is a relationship that is very much in sync. This pair also benefits each other because you are compatible. Neither of you carry heavy emotional baggage towards the other, and there are no hidden agendas between you. Your element profile does not indicate superlative luck for either of you, but you make do with what you have.

In terms of afflictions, both of you have to cope with some ill feng shui winds. The Monkey has the illness star, while the Rooster is forced to confront the *Three Killings*, which causes it to expend its energy; it also has to subdue the *Violence Star 7* which has flown into its home direction.

The planning and strategic skills of the Monkey reflect those of the Rooster, so the relationship is strengthening to both signs. This is a pairing that improves as both mature, although do not expect lifelong total fidelity. Both of you tend to have roving eyes. But for both, making a commitment to one another does hold real meaning. You are strong personalities, so your commitment to one another is serious when given.

MONKEY WITH DOG
In 2013, attraction here sparks creativity and a happy outcome

The Monkey and Dog have an uncomplicated relationship. Here, the Dog will almost always bow to the leadership of the Monkey, and if romance brings the two of you together, it will last even if the Monkey can be a challenge to the Dog.

We see here a vivacious sign (the Monkey) that can be very flirtatious romantically, getting together with a loyal long-suffering kind of personality. The Dog thinks long-term, more so than the Monkey. In 2013, the Dog is very strong and focused and also very lucky. These two signs have a big disparity in their vitality levels and in the way they view themselves.

Generally, the Monkey dominates this relationship, but in 2013, it is the Dog who will be the stronger of the two. It will be the vitality of the Dog that will fuel this relationship.

This is because the Dog's Life Force and Inner Essence are at a maximum level, making it strong and full of vitality. The Dog also has great self assurance and the Monkey is genuinely attracted then to the glow and charisma of the Dog personality. The Monkey will actively seek out a relationship because the Dog's confidence is infectious, and quite rightly so, as it is the kind that stems from sitting on the *Star of Small Auspicious*, with the *Star of Big Auspicious* on its left coming from the Boar direction. That these stars are brought by the 24 Mountain Compass are strong indications of potential good fortune.

The Monkey will be more than aware that this is a match that is beneficial and will therefore pursue it with great enthusiasm.

The Monkey will enjoy loyalty and dedication from the Dog, although this is something you do not fully appreciate and will often overlook. The Monkey is not known for its sensitivity. Nevertheless, the Dog sign stays satisfied and happy with the Monkey, so this is a good match.

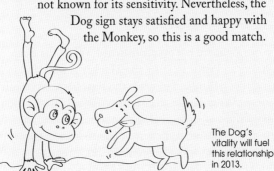

The Dog's vitality will fuel this relationship in 2013.

MONKEY WITH BOAR

In 2013, Boar's charisma wins over the Monkey

A match with the Boar in a love relationship will definitely benefit the Monkey in 2013, as the Boar brings some truly excellent luck energies.

Not only does the Boar have strong Life Force and Inner Essence, this sign is also flanked by Stars of Big Auspicious on either side of its home location on the compass. This causes the Boar to be surrounded by good energy vibrations that will easily rub off on anyone getting close. The Monkey is thus certain to benefit from being around the Boar.

When it comes to vitality and inner essence however, the two signs are not evenly matched. While the Boar is strong and virile in 2013, the Monkey is weak and in fact rather lethargic. But while the Boar has a very weak personal Wind Horse, the Monkey's Wind Horse luck is powerful and strong, being at maximum levels. The two signs therefore complement one another in terms of their element and luck profile in 2013. Your signs are both fun loving, but in 2013, the Monkey's expectations of the Boar may be unrealistic. As partners in business or as professionals working together, their temperaments are totally compatible.

Work-wise therefore, there could be a mismatch of inputs and expectations. The Boar does not expect to contribute much in terms of effort. And the Monkey is definitely not a workaholic in 2013. As far as the love dimension of their relationship goes the two signs can also be out of sync. But in 2013 the Boar's charisma wins over the Monkey!

Note that the Boar sits on the *Star of the Sui Po* - which can be exhausting and there is danger of excesses. With this sign also enjoying the heavenly star of 6, it is easy for the Boar to over indulge. Hopefully you can add a sense of balance into the relationship.

> Your two signs may not be totally compatible, but as long as a **win-win situation** prevails the relationship works.

In 2013, you can both win BIG with the Monkey tapping into the Boar's double *Big Auspicious*. With your powerful Wind Horse and the Boar's auspicious feng shui winds to fuel the relationship, both sides will surely benefit.

PART FIVE

IMPROVING MONKEY'S FENG SHUI IN 2013

1. Subduing Illness Affliction
   In Monkey's Southwest Location
2. Making The Most Of The Monkey's Lucky Directions
3. Boosting Monkey's Wealth Luck In 2013
4. Maintaining Your Vitality & Life Essence
5. Enhancing Your "Windhorse" or Lung Ta
6. Presence of the Power Elephant
7. High Potency Three Harmony Warriors Mirror
8. Five Sense Tools of Enjoyment
9. Regular Incense Offerings

The Monkey enjoys quite the bonanza year when things just fall unexpectedly into place for you! You find yourself swinging from month to month picking fruits from magic trees quite effortlessly, and accomplish success almost without having to do much at all. The Monkey had it a little rough last year, having to cope with such a lot of angry vibes coming from the 3 as well as two conflict stars flanking you. But thankfully this is now over, and 2013 promises a more pleasant and exciting ride.

A big source of your great good fortune this year comes from the patronage of the *Heaven Seal Star* that has flown into your astrological palace. The cosmic realms are definitely smiling at you, as the **God of Heaven** bestows his seal of authority to the Monkey-born this year. With this seal, many obstacles can be easily dispelled, and help from the cosmos are despatched whenever aid is needed. Thus the Monkey who wants to succeed this year **must possess the Heaven Seal at all times**. This is the first tip to creating gold for you this year.

The lucky Monkey enters the Year of the Snake, whom as you know is your secret friend. Your astrological connection with the Snake is an exceptionally auspicious one, a partnership that yields abundance as well as offering the prospect of elevating your rank in life. So for the career Monkey, your work life takes a leap forward and you can expect to be offered a flashier title and given more authority. For the Monkey in business, a lucrative deal is indicated in the charts, possibly a "once-in-a-lifetime"-type opportunity to make it big! There is money to be made in 2013, as Wealth luck looks rosy for all Monkeys, with the exception of the **57 year old Fire Monkey** whose cash flow will be a little tight. But not to worry as this something that can be alleviated with some clever feng shui therapy.

Single Monkeys looking for love will also find happiness in this area. As an animal sign who occupies the Southwest palace in the Zodiac, romance luck is already latent in your birth chart! No doubt you already have a string of willing partners; the problem is which one to choose! Meeting the right one isn't always easy for the Monkey-born, but in 2013, your love luck turns from casual romance into something more serious, as the number 2 returns to its original position in the Lo Shu square!

If getting married is top of your mind this year, then wear a locket that features the **Double Happiness Symbol** - this will help in matters concerning meeting your soulmate. **Married Monkeys** enjoy a surge of happiness luck in family life.

The motherly side of Monkey matriarchs will bubble up in full force this year, and you find yourself focusing your attention more and more towards nurturing your little ones. The year of the Snake (your secret friend) is also an excellent year to **get pregnant** or **adopt a child** if you wish to expand your family unit; a Snake baby will definitely bring so much joy and add to your already very lucky platter!

The Snake Year serves up quite a delightful spread for the Monkey, but the only thing that spoils your psychic appetite is the lack of zeal to rise to the occasion! It is not your fault really, as the feng shui chart does bring illness winds with the number 2 star flying into your palace in the **Southwest**.

Fortunately, the Monkey's health luck is fairly stable across the board, and this will help a great deal towards supressing long-term or terminal illness. The Monkey who enjoys the best health in 2013 is the **33 year old Metal Monkey**, but the **57 year old Fire Monkey** does have very low health luck this year and will need to implement some strong feng shui element therapy to fortify his/her health luck.

With illness energies bringing you down, the Monkey's usual confidence in pursuing life's adventures takes a dip and you will find yourself wallowing in thoughts of self-doubt, particularly in the earlier months of the year when your energies are not so vibrant. Your characteristic enthusiasm is replaced with moodiness, and depression gets the better of you due to the presence of the *Yin House Star* coming from the left hand side of the 24 Mountains Chart.

When the Yin House appears, this normally indicates some kind of misfortune manifesting in a very yin way. In a bad feng shui month, i.e. when the illness 2, 5 yellow or violent 7 strikes your **Southwest** palace or into your bedroom, you could meet with a minor accident or encounter a near-death incident.

But most of the time the Yin House indicates the likelihood of being affected by yin situations happening around you i.e. a member of your family or someone close to you taking ill or passing away this year. Hence the presence of the Yin House usually leads to the onset of a fragile emotional state, making you more vulnerable to mental disturbances and illness.

As both your Spirit Essence and Vitality are very low, you are indeed quite exposed to this star, and thus MUST adopt the necessary feng shui precautions to stay protected. Our advice is to install a strong spiritual feng shui cure that can control this malevolent star.

For example, the **White Umbrella Goddess** is the ultimate matriarchal goddess figure for overcoming physical and spirit harm, and she is best placed in the Southwest to subdue the Yin House. You may display her image engraved on a plaque or etched on a crystal ball. For personal protection it is also an excellent idea to wear her **OM heart syllable** as a pendant, or a suitably consecrated amulet which you can wear on our body wherever you go.

But other than your tendency to feel a little off-weather and catch an illness during the bad months, the Monkey really has great potential of making 2013 a stand-out year. With the *Heaven Seal Star* on your side and your strong Wind Horse Luck this year, **the key** to making it big is to enhance all your lucky corners of the house, and subdue all the negative stars.

You should feel really excited that all these goodies are in store for you and put effort into strengthening both your Vitality and your Spirit Essence, as these are the only two areas that are weak in your chart. In other categories of luck, you are endowed with strong Success Luck and very good Wealth Luck, both of which indicate that that achieving your goals will happen without needing too much hard work from you!

This very unique luck pattern is seldom enjoyed by other animal signs so focus your mind towards keeping your feng shui up-to-date and you'll have everything you need to shine quite brilliantly this year! Make all the necessary adjustments in your placement of symbolic energizers in all the eight corners of your living areas and be extra mindful to subdue the **Five Yellow** in the centre location of your living room. By doing this you ensure that the energy of all afflicted sectors in your living spaces are properly taken care of and all the good sectors are well activated!

More importantly, keep your outlook fresh and upbeat by strengthening your vitality and spirit essence. By implementing these feng shui techniques, you will accumulate the stamina and confidence needed to reap all the goodies coming your way this year!

SUBDUING THE ILLNESS AFFLICTION OF THE MONKEY'S SOUTHWEST LOCATION
Keeping the 2 subdued to ensure an illness-free year

The first thing every Monkey needs to do each New Year is to check its own home location which is Southwest. With any luck, this part of your home should not be occupied by either the toilet or the store

room. If it is occupied by a toilet, it seriously damages
your luck and your energy. To ensure the Monkey's
luck is not blocked, the **Southwest** corners of
bedrooms, work rooms and other important rooms in
the house should not be cluttered with old newspapers
or any build-up of carelessly discarded stuff. This can
happen in any home, and that is why it is so necessary
to undertake a good clean-up just prior to every New
Year. Rooms that get excessively cluttered cause *yin chi*
to build up.

Space feng shui can only be lucky when chi energy
can flow unimpeded. When blockages are there, they
almost always cause various aspects of your life to get
stalled. Remember the **Southwest** is also the palace
of the Matriarch and when this is clogged or afflicted
by a toilet or a storeroom, marriage luck can really
suffer, leading to family breakups and couples splitting
up. The luck of the Mother is also adversely affected
and this weakens her position in the family unit, and
tarnishes her career prospects at work. Thus family
happiness is very much governed by the state of the
Southwest and this is why it is so vital that this area
of the house is not blocked or left in a chaotic state of
mess.

For the Monkey-born, an untidy Southwest will certainly magnify the illness effects of the 2 causing illness to plague both the Monkey-born and the Matriarch of the household. Hence the Southwest needs to be kept clear, and the illness star there needs to be subdued.

In 2013, the Monkey has a mixed bag of good and bad indications from the charts we are analysing.

- Firstly, the Monkey enjoys an auspicious connection with the Snake Year, being its secret friend. This partnership brings abundance and upward mobility for the Monkey's career or business.

- In the feng shui chart, the Monkey's Southwest location is being visited by the *Illness 2 Star*, which can lead to extreme fatigue, recurrent sickness, or in a worst-case scenario, contracting a fatal disease. Luckily, the Monkey has stable health luck in 2013 but subduing the 2 is none-the-less very vital.

- On the 24 Mountains Compass chart, the Monkey sits on the *Heaven Seal Star*, which brings the patronage of the **God of Heaven,** something special that can almost override all other afflictions. Displaying this seal ensures that the Monkey captures maximum benefit from it.

- Lastly, the Monkey has the *Yin House Star* coming from the left which could trigger a yin episode in the Monkey's life. Strong cosmic protection is needed to subdue this star and protect the Monkey from falling victim to spirit harm.

For these reasons, the Monkey should really pay attention to ensuring that your personal feng shui is safeguarded this year. The good news is that by knowing feng shui and understanding the nature of these stars, you can greatly enhance your good stars and improve on the less favourable indications using element therapy and wearing targeted amulets to increase your personal chi. Luck is always about balancing the chi forces, and thus feng shui arms you with the knowledge to subdue the negative and amplify the positives!

First, start by ensuring your home location in the Southwest is kept well-enhanced with good element compatibility. In the cycle of elements, you need the power of Metal to exhaust the hostile 2 and strengthen your intrinsic Monkey element, but metal will also exhaust your Southwest location whose home element is earth. So here we recommend that you place the powerful **Golden Longevity Vase** to supress the 2, but at the same time install yellow-coloured crystal balls here to nourish the **Southwest** location and keep it strong.

It is also very interesting to note that based on the year's element chart for 2013, the element of Metal brings supportive friends and Earth brings Resource luck in this year's chart. Activating Metal and Earth in the Southwest thus brings the luck of allies as well as resources on your side, and together these greatly strengthens your personal energies for 2013.

Another way to keeping the Monkey well supported is to bring in the luck of the Monkey's allies. For this you can invite the image of the **Dragon, Rat** and the **Snake** and place them in the Southwest location. The Snake, who is the Monkey's secret friend, is one of the best allies the Monkey can have in 2013.

As mentioned in earlier chapters the Monkey and the Snake form a powerful bond that can literally catapult your lifestyle into new heights! The Snake enjoys a spectacular year in 2013 so joining forces with this sign benefits the Monkey tremendously. If you already have a spouse or a family member who is a Snake, then you are already benefitting from this very auspicious match. Otherwise, it makes sense to cosy-up with a Snake person this year, or carry the image of the Snake with you always as a **keychain charm** or **pendant**.

Leaning on the strengths of your other allies are also very beneficial as both your competitive allies the Rat and the Dragon have super strong charts this year. The Rat has high luck ratings in almost every category of its personal chart; high ratings for Success, Wealth, Spirit Essence and Life Force, and is flanked by two Big Auspicious Stars. Just by associating with the Rat, your propensity for good luck increases by leaps.

The Dragon is also equally lucky and equally robust in all its personal chi areas and being friends with the fearless Dragon will lift your confidence almost instantly! So for the Monkey we highly recommend inviting the images of the **Rat** and the **Dragon,** or carry images of them as little charms, or paste decals of them in your **Southwest**.

During the Autumn season, you can also benefit from your two seasonal friends the **Rooster** and the **Dog**, who both enjoy excellent Spirit Essence and Vitality in 2013. Wear the **Friends of Autumn Scarf** around your neck or in your chest pocket to borrow their luck, as this will add to your inner stamina and help you overcome your health obstacles.

In a year where illness and yin energies hover around you, creating auspicious vibes by piggy-backing on the luck of stronger allies will go very far in fortifying your inner and outer constitution, making your luck complete in 2013.

YOUR PERSONAL LUCKY DIRECTIONS
Fine-tuning auspicious directions for the Monkey in 2013

Every year, the energies of the eight main directions of the compass transform bringing a change of luck in every sector. Keeping track of these changing chi energies is the underlying basis for maintaining good feng shui in any new year. This applies equally to the different sectors of the home as well as to enhance your own personal luck. The latter involves being mindful of your directions when you are sitting, sleeping or directly facing someone while talking or interacting.

Not staying updated on the lucky and unlucky directions of each New Year can cause you to experience a sudden and unpleasant reversal of fortune!

Using and making the most of one's lucky directions is one of the easiest ways of tapping into the good feng shui of the year. However these lucky and unlucky directions are influenced by the year's energies and must be fine-tuned.

Lucky and unlucky directions are divided into EAST and WEST directions. The EAST directions are East, Southeast, North and South while the WEST directions are West, Northwest, Southwest and Northeast.

So depending on whether you are an East or West person, one set of directions will be beneficial and the other set non-beneficial. And just as there are East and West people, there are also East and West houses, rooms, corners and so forth. In feng shui, everything that has to do with direction or location is categorised according to whether it is East or West.

West people always do better, live better and are happier when using West directions, spaces and locations. For them, all the East directions and locations are unlucky for them. The same goes for those who are East people, for whom East directions hold special positive influences for them and West directions generally bring ill winds.

> However, from year to year, all directions are affected by the changing energies of the year. Knowing how your lucky directions are affected is part of the updating and fine-tuning process.

Sitting in your good luck directions, and facing a direction that also brings you luck, are the best ways of attracting excellent feng shui when you need it most i.e. when making a sales pitch, negotiating a raise or when you are trying to impress someone and making and important proposal. Those are times when you really need, and thus, benefit from good feng shui winds.

When one goes through a mixed year like what the Monkey is going through, facing your SUCCESS direction adds weight to your lucky platter and reduces the bad effects of the unlucky stars. During bad years, sitting in and facing your good fortune directions can also help you ward off afflictive energy within your home and work environments.

In any kind of year, you should avoid facing any one of your four unlucky directions i.e. East directions if you are a West person, and West directions if you an East person.

The table at the following pages summarises the good luck directions for all those born in Monkey years based on their heavenly stem and their gender. Take note of your lucky directions! Sitting in one's good luck directions is one of the most fundamental of feng shui practices. When one goes through a good year, doing this correctly will ensure that all the good energy is efficiently "captured". During bad years, sitting in one's good fortune directions will ensure that one is insulated from setbacks and misfortunes.

AUSPICIOUS DIRECTIONS
for Monkey Men

YEAR OF BIRTH/AGE	HS ELEMENT	SUCCESS DIRECTION	HEALTH DIRECTION	LOVE DIRECTION	PERSONAL GROWTH DIRECTION
1944/69 YEARS	Wood Monkey	NE ★	West ♪	NW	SW ✚
1956/57 YEARS	Fire Monkey	SW ✚	NW	West ♪	NE ★
1968/45 YEARS	Earth Monkey	NE ★	West ♪	NW	SW ✚
1980/33 YEARS	Metal Monkey	NE ★	West ♪	NW	SW ✚
1992/21 YEARS	Water Monkey	SW ✚	NW	West ♪	NE ★
2004/9 YEARS	Wood Monkey	NE ★	West ♪	NW	SW ✚

✚ Shows illness afflicted direction in 2013

♪ Afflicted by violence & betrayal star

⚡ Afflicted by quarrelsome star

★ Direction is enjoying excellent feng shui luck in 2013

AUSPICIOUS DIRECTIONS
for Monkey Women

YEAR OF BIRTH/AGE	HS ELEMENT	SUCCESS DIRECTION	HEALTH DIRECTION	LOVE DIRECTION	PERSONAL GROWTH DIRECTION
1944/69 YEARS	Wood Monkey	North	South	East ⚡	SE
1956/57 YEARS	Fire Monkey	NW	SW ➕	NE ★	West ⌒
1968/45 YEARS	Earth Monkey	SE	East ⚡	South	North
1980/33 YEARS	Metal Monkey	North	South	East ⚡	SE
1992/21 YEARS	Water Monkey	NW	SW ➕	NE ★	West ⌒
2004/9 YEARS	Wood Monkey	SE	East ⚡	South	North

➕ Shows illness afflicted direction in 2013

⌒ Afflicted by violence & betrayal star

⚡ Afflicted by quarrelsome star

★ Direction is enjoying excellent feng shui luck in 2013

Next take note of the following afflicted directions and try to avoid using these directions in 2013 even though are "lucky directions for you". They may be lucky for you based on the formula but this year they are afflicted:

WEST people please avoid directly facing these lucky directions of yours:
• **Southwest** because this direction is afflicted by illness winds (unless you have placed the cure)
• **West** because facing this direction attracts betrayal and dishonesty luck

EAST people avoid directly facing these lucky directions of yours:
• **East** because facing this direction causes aggravation, misunderstandings and hostility to get created between you and anyone you may be interacting with.

In 2013, the West directions of Northeast and Northwest are very auspicious, and for the Monkey men and women who belong to the WEST group, you might want to try and face either of these two directions. The **Northeast** enjoys the money bringing number 8 which spells prosperity. **Gentlemen Monkeys** born in the lunar years of **1944, 1968, 1980** and **2004** will enjoy what we Chinese Hokkien term as "*chia beh liao*" which means "more than enough to eat" as facing this direction brings you both prosperity and excellent Success Luck! The **Northwest** direction is also very auspicious as it enjoys the heavenly number 6 in 2013. For the **57 year old gentleman Monkey,** this direction also brings you much needed Health luck which will help fortify your cosmic immune system against illness winds brought by the 2 this year.

The Northwest is also excellent for all West Group Monkey ladies as this facing direction has the added benefit of bringing you Sheng Chi, which is your Success luck.

For Monkey ladies who belong to the East group, it would benefit you to face the North or the South directions throughout the year, because not only are these two directions good for you, they also enjoy lucky star numbers in 2013. Both these directions are flanked by the stars of *Big and Small Auspicious* on either side of them. Plus the South enjoys the completion future prosperity winds of the 9 and North enjoys the winds of victory brought by the 1.

Wood Monkey and **Metal Monkey ladie**s have an extra reason to face North this year, as this also happens to be their *Sheng Chi* direction which is their personal Success Luck direction. This direction brings abundance of auspicious good fortune in business and in careers.

IMPORTANT: Where facing directions are concerned, please take note of the "facing taboos" of each year, as this overrides the East/West formula of directions. Southeast 3 plays host to the **Grand Duke Jupiter** this year and facing this direction will incur his wrath. Do not face Southeast 3 even this direction is one of your four good directions. This applies particularly to East Group Monkeys where Southeast is either their Success or Personal Growth direction; for this year, face North or South instead. Also remember that the *Three Killings* has flown into the East in 2013 and to avert bad luck from this malicious star you must not sit with your back facing the East this year; this means all West group Monkeys should also **avoid facing West** this year.

SUGGESTIONS OF APPLYING GOOD LUCK DIRECTIONS
At the Office

The sketches below show the best way of arranging your desk at the office. The arrows indicate your facing direction **and this should correspond to one of your lucky directions,** preferably your SUCCESS direction and even better if in 2013 you take note of the foregoing advice i.e. West Monkey try to tap Northwest and Northeast and East Monkey try to tap North or South as their facing direction for work. Just using these correct directions is sufficient to bring you BIG and positive changes in your success luck!

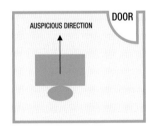
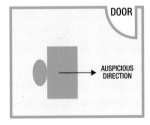

Note that you should never have your back towards the door, and that the best place for your desk is diagonally across the room from the door into the room.

At Home

Having determined the lucky directions you can use to improve your feng shui in 2013, you can start looking at your bedroom, your dining area and your work area to see how you can adjust your furniture to enable you to capture your lucky feng shui directions. You should do this as early in the year as possible. It is worth the effort to do so as the direction you sleep, eat or work really does make a huge difference to your overall and general well-being. We are not talking only about generating Success Luck but also creating a feeling of wellness and serenity. Good feng shui always brings a feeling of relaxed fulfillment and restfulness to your personal environment.

There are several ways to use your lucky personal directions in the home. The challenge is to do so without inadvertently getting hit by a secret poison arrow, such as a sharp corner or a big cupboard or pillar.

In the Bedroom

Always try to sleep with your head pointing to one of your lucky directions. If your bed is already pointed to a lucky direction but in 2013 is afflicted, i.e. if it is pointed to the East, Southwest or West, then it might be worthwhile to try rearranging your bed to point to another lucky direction this year. So for example, last year the West was favourable prosperity luck, but in 2013 it is afflicted with the 7 star and thus you should find an alternative lucky direction for sleeping this year.

The way to capture the sleeping direction effectively is to note the direction the top of your head is pointed to when you are lying down on the bed. This is the direction which should be auspicious for you.

Do not use the feet's pointing direction, as this is in incorrect way of applying this formula.

Note that while getting your sleeping direction correct, there are other guidelines to follow when arranging the bedroom.

Try to arrange your furniture such that the positioning of the bed is not directly hit by exposed overhead beams, protruding corners or mirrors reflecting the bed. Do not have the bed directly in the line of doors or share a wall with a toilet on the other side of the wall. Follow these guidelines seriously. Try to capture a good

sleeping direction while observing these bedroom
pointers.

Also take note that, if you are sleeping in the corner
that corresponds to your home direction (for the
Monkey it is Southwest) you will enjoy a more restful
sleep each night. But this year since Southwest
is afflicted with the illness 2, for the Monkey we
recommend choosing another corner that isn't so
sickly. For example, you can also use the corners that
correspond to your **astrological allies** or **secret friend**
direction.

For the Monkey, remember that your allies are the
Rat (North 2) and the Dragon (Southeast 1) and your
secret friend is the Snake (Southeast 3). In 2013 all
your two allies and friend the Snake are blessed with
auspicious stars, and so you may consider sleeping any
of these corners of your bedroom.

One location usually worth avoiding is the direction
of your "enemy", and for the Monkey this is the Tiger
corner in the Northeast. However in 2013 this "taboo"
can be safely ignored as the energy of the Southwest
creates the auspicious *sum-of-ten* combination with
the Northeast direction.

Toilet door or kitchen door should not face the bed

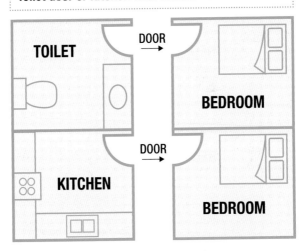

Furniture should not be pointing to the bed

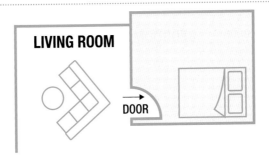

Bed should be placed deep inside the bedroom

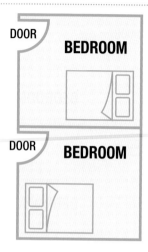

The best way to position the bed within the bedroom is to have the bed as far in as possible.

Leave a gap between the bed and the window

Don't have your bed right next to the window, as this is like you are "falling out". When you go to sleep is when you are most vulnerable.

Bed must not face the door

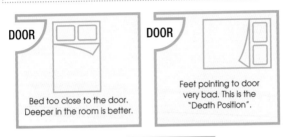

DOOR

Bed too close to the door.
Deeper in the room is better.

DOOR

Feet pointing to door
very bad. This is the
"Death Position".

DOOR

Bed is too near
the door here.

Bed must not be below an exposed beam

DOOR

This will give rise to
headaches, migraines
and sleepless nights.

Exposed beam

Avoid placing a TV facing the bed

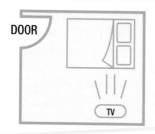

A TV in the bedroom can act as a mirror causing harm to the marriage, and will also affect how well you can sleep.

Avoid having mirrors on your wardrobe reflecting your bed

wardrobe with mirror doors

Having exposed mirrors in the bedroom will make it difficult for you to have a good night's sleep and can also cause bad dreams and nightmares, as well as third party interference to the marriage.

Remember that the Northeast also enjoys the prosperity 8 this year! Hence if you really cannot place your bed in any of your allies or friends corners, then in 2013 the Northeast also brings excellent luck for the placement of your bed and furniture.

BOOSTING THE MONKEY'S WEALTH LUCK IN 2013
Using element therapy to activate the luck of material prosperity

Each year there is an element of the year that indicates **Wealth Luck**, and this element interacts with your own wealth element, which is determined according to the year you were born. This is the abbreviated version of investigating one's wealth luck according to one's animal sign.

This method of element analysis was extremely popular during the times of the Tang Emperors, a period of Chinese history when feng shui was very much at the peak of its popularity especially under the Empress *Wu Tze Tien*. Much of the astrological tables and calculations also made their way to Tibet which during those times enjoyed good relations with China. Indeed, the Tibet King was married to the *Tang princess Wen Cheng* who brought many of China's esoteric knowledge with her to Tibet.

Focusing on enhancing the Monkey's wealth luck is not difficult once you know how your personal wealth element interacts with the wealth element of the year. Each year, you have to see how weak or strong your wealth luck is, and then use element therapy to strengthen your wealth element. The wealth element for each of the Monkey-born is different, as this has to be extracted from the lineage tables.

The Wealth luck element of the different Monkey people in 2013 and what needs to be done by each type of Monkey are summarised here:

HEAVENLY STEM /AGE IN 2013	WEALTH ELEMENT	WEALTH ELEMENT OF 2013	Quality of Wealth Luck in 2013 & How to Enhance your Wealth Luck i.e. strengthen it
WOOD MONKEY/ 69 YEARS	WOOD	WATER	000 - excellent. No need to do anything!
FIRE MONKEY/ 57 YEARS	FIRE	WATER	XX - very low. Increase WOOD energy around you.
EARTH MONKEY/ 45 YEARS	EARTH	WATER	00 - very good. Increase FIRE energy around you.
METAL MONKEY/ 33 YEARS	METAL	WATER	OX - neutral. Increase Earth Energy around you.
WATER MONKEY/ 21 YEARS	WATER	WATER	0 - good. Increase METAL energy around you.
WOOD MONKEY/ 9 YEARS	WOOD	WATER	000 - excellent. No need to do anything!

To enhance your Wealth Luck according to the element luck formula, take note of which element you need to increase in order to strengthen the quality of your wealth luck. If you need not do anything, then please do follow our advice, as feng shui is about harmony. This is the case with the **69 year old Wood Monkey,** who enjoys the best of wealth luck in 2013.

If your wealth luck is already at its height, increasing the element to enhance your wealth element can transform good luck into bad luck. Then instead of bringing you happiness and harmony, it could instead cause you aggravation, worry and even severe repercussions.

For all the other Monkeys, using element therapy can greatly enhance your ability to capturing wealth this year, and for those at least one **X** in their luck rating, strengthening your wealth luck can help guard against the reversal of fortune. For example, the **33 year old Metal Monkey** and the **57 year old Fire Monkey** both have **X** in their wealth luck and this indicates that financial matters will be a source of anxiety for you. Just follow the guide in the following pages on how to use element therapy to correct these energy imbalances:

INCREASING WOOD ENERGY means displaying more plants near you. These should look lush and be growing well. Never have diseased or dying plants near you – there is nothing that emits worse feng shui than this.

INCREASING FIRE ENERGY means turning on more and brighter lights. Note that yellow golden light is better than white fluorescent lights. Make your house more yang than yin!

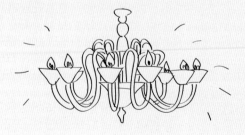

INCREASING EARTH ENERGY means surrounding your immediate environment with auspicious symbols made of stone/earth/crystals such as porcelain vases, crystal balls and so forth.

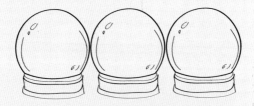

INCREASING METAL ENERGY means hanging metal windchimes that create the sounds of metal around you. Choose auspicious windchimes that emit pleasing sounds. This will strengthen the Water element that is your wealth element. Please note that the chimes must be all-metal, as this is an element enhancer.

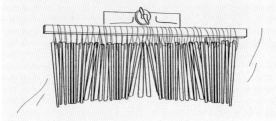

INCREASING WATER ENERGY means placing water features near you. Here the water should be moving to generate live "yang" water. An aquarium or small zen fountain will do very nicely.

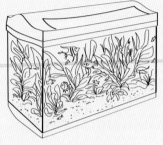

MAINTAINING YOUR VITALITY & LIFE ESSENCE
Strengthening internal stamina to overcome negative vibes

In the same way that you need to increase the presence of one of the five elements to enhance your Wealth luck, you can also use auspicious element therapy to increase your *Vitality* and *Spirit Essence*. These two chi energies combined is what brings you the feel-good energy to enjoy life and withstand any difficulties that you have to face each year.

There is no point in being rich and successful if you are simply feeling too ill or too "blah" to even bother! When your vitality is weak, it has to do with the energies affecting you in any year. Sometimes vitality gets sapped when the cosmic spirits around us feel neglected and this is why we recommend everyone to offer incense via joss sticks or by burning special appeasement incense!

All those born in the year of the Monkey have METAL as their Vitality element, and in 2013, the Vitality element of the year is Fire. In the cycle of element compatibility, Fire destroys Metal, and hence the Monkey's vitality or life force is severely impaired in 2013.

Essentially this means that your internal stamina is at its lowest point, your chakra energies are very weak, and thus you feel depressed and demotivated about life. To remedy this, you need to increase the presence of **Earth** to produce and strengthen your **Metal.** Place **crystal balls** near you, on your desk at work, or in the Southwest. The best are crystal balls etched with powerful images like the **White Umbrella Goddess** who protects against illness caused by disease or poisons.

The other aspect of your chi force which is also low is your *Spirit Essence*. All Monkeys have Earth as their Spirit Essence element, and in 2013 the year's Spirit essence element is **Wood**. In the cycle of element compatibility, Wood completely saps the vital energies of **Earth**, and thus your Spirit Essence is also weakened considerably. To remedy this you need increased Fire energy around you to produce more Earth. Thus it is a good idea to keep your home well-lit in 2013 and in particular it would help to shine a table lamp on the **White Umbrella Goddess Crystal Ball** placed on your desk. Doing this will simultaneously strengthen both your Life force and your Spirit Essence together. In addition to this, make regular incense offerings to the local deities and landlords, and your spirit essence will gain further strength! Implementing these simple suggestions will lift your confidence, nurture you spiritually and fortify you sufficiently to withstand any obstacles brought by the **Yin House**.

The White Umbrella Goddess strengthens your Spirit Essence and protects you from spirit dangers.

ENHANCING YOUR "WINDHORSE" OR LUNG TA
Keeping Success Luck overflowing throughout the year

Success Luck is brought to you by your Wind Horse which carries the powerful energies of your mind. Its strength varies from year to year, but to those who are adept at spiritual meditations, they have the ability to seriously empower themselves by increasing the strength of their inner Wind Horse and when strong, the Wind Horse can even lend strength and support for the other four categories of luck that determine well-being each year.

When the Wind Horse is weak, bad luck can strike suddenly and unexpectedly UNLESS it is swiftly overcome. There are many ways to compensate for a weak Wind Horse.

A very popular way, especially with the Tibetans who have transformed this astrological cure into a religious practice, is by hanging prayer flags with the image and mantra of the Wind Horse high above their homes. This custom and practice has in recent years become very popular.

According to the texts, just having the **image of the Wind Horse** placed in the highest part of the house is usually good enough to compensate for any residents' weak personal Wind Horse. Thus having an image of the Wind Horse in the house, especially when displayed in the upper levels or on the roof even, will increase Success luck for everyone within.

When your Windhorse is strong, you are said then to be able to "fly through the air, riding a white horse enjoying the auspicious winds of the cosmic environment..."

For the Monkey-born, your Wind Horse is flying very high this year! Your personal Wind Horse element at the time of your birth was **Wood**. In 2013, the year's Wind Horse element is **Water** which nourishes and produces your Wind Horse. This means that in 2013 those born in a Monkey year enjoy the fruits of Success quite effortlessly despite your low energies in other areas! To ensure your Wind Horse luck is maintained robust throughout the year, invite the image of a **Bejewelled Wind Horse** that is empowered with its own mantras. This will ensure that your Wind Horse luck remains stable and all other obstacles are kept at bay!

PRESENCE OF THE POWER ELEPHANT
Channelling Power Luck from the heavens through the Elephant

The Monkey is indeed blessed by having the lucky *Heaven Seal Star* firmly in its palace. The presence of this powerful star indicates help from a divine source, signifying that any obstacles that prevent your good fortune can be overcome. The God of Heaven lends you his seal of authority for the year and thus it would be wise to display the **Seal of Heaven** prominently in the Southwest to establish your position of power!

In a year where you also have the *Side Three Killing*s on the right hand side to deal with, your influence in the work place could be challenged by colleagues who are less supportive of your easy success. The *Side Three Killing*s normally manifests three types of misfortune i.e. the loss of good name, loss of relationships and also the loss of money.

The good news is that the *Side Three Killings* is easily subdued simply by "facing" it head-on. This means willing your mind to stay resilient and commanding, and by strengthening your power and effectiveness, you will also increase your endurance to ward off conflict energies that sap your energy for the year.

In astrological feng shui, although the mighty elephant is not one of the twelve animals of the Zodiac wheel, it is nevertheless considered a sacred beast which signifies **power** and **authority**. The elephant features in many of the sacred legends and stories of Eastern traditions; and in countries such as India and Thailand, the elephant, and especially the white elephant, is revered as a sacred beast.

The white elephant is the precious elephant which carries the wish granting jewel on its back. It is similar to the white Wind Horse, but where the Horse brings success, the elephant brings power. For the Monkey, having **a pair of precious white elephants**, one with the trunk up and the other with the trunk down, is the best way of ensuring the luck of **Heaven Seal star** manifests in a timely and fruitful manner for you. It also ensures that there will be fewer obstacles causing problems. So for 2013, invite a pair of white elephants and to place them in the Southwest sector of the home.

HIGH POTENCY THREE HARMONY WARRIORS MIRROR
Keeping jealousy vibes and hostility under control

One of the aggravating occurrences that will disturb your peace of mind is the unfortunate assault of perfidious gossip and jealous talk which often rears its ugly head in the calculating arena of office politics. Nothing is more exhausting than having to put up with fair-weathered co-workers who smile at your presence and stab you when your back is turned. This unfortunately is the negative effect of being blessed with success that comes so easily for you, and in 2013 this becomes exacerbated with the *Side Three Killings* coming from your right side of the 24 Mountains Chart.

When you are on the roll, others will look upon your achievements with envious eyes. For those watching you, every little thing you do (or don't do) becomes fuel for the gossip mills! The most likely place where this quickly turns into something harmful is at the work place. It is a good idea to preempt the situation by carrying a very unique and powerful cure that combines the power of Fire element (to subdue hostility) with the three powerful tools that combat disharmony. This should keep all jealous feelings under control.

This is the **Three Harmony Warriors Mirror** finished with red enamel on one side and featuring the three symbols of victory in the fight against disharmony on the other. This would be the 8 legged lion, the fur bearing fish and the sea conch dragon. They are sacred guardians that successfully keep all envy, anger and hostility at bay.

This Three Harmony Warriors Mirror when displayed in your home can also subdue abusive behavior, reduce sibling rivalry, and generally create a harmonious environment. In the office, this is a powerful remedy for reducing office rivalry and subduing petty politicking. The presence of these three creatures also promotes cooperation and teamwork in the office.

FIVE SENSE TOOLS OF ENJOYMENT
Ensuring perfect balance of all five senses of enjoyment

The Chinese believe that all good fortune manifests in eight kinds of luck, which can be enhanced when powerful symbols are displayed in each of eight direction corners of the house. These are:

- continuous good health and long life
- asset wealth that keeps growing,
- good flow of income which does not end
- stable family environment; a good marriage
- filial descendents; good sons and daughters
- good name respected by many
- wisdom and good mental ability
- patronage of kings and noblemen

But to enjoy manifestations of good fortune continuously, we need the five tools of enjoyment. Learned feng shui Masters would always ensure that households under their care have the **five sense tools of enjoyment** in their homes as these represent the assurance that the household residents, and especially the Patriarch, can enjoy the eight manifestations of good fortune. It is really very kiasu of course, but this actually is the heart of good feng shui – create the cause for good things to happen and they will!

For the coming Year of the Snake, all homes can benefit from these five things which symbolize the five sense awareness:

- **MIRROR** for an abundance of beautiful things
- **LUTE** so you are soothed by enchanting sounds
- **INCENSE** so your heart is at peace
- **FRUIT** to symbolize feasting through life
- **SILK GARMENT** to symbolize the softness of your beautiful robes

REGULAR
INCENSE OFFERINGS
Appeasing local landlords for a stress free year

An effective way to ensure a smooth year with nothing to disturb your well being, and to ensure you and those in your household are free of accidents, illness and problems caused by outside forces such as falling victim to people with bad intentions – burning and offering incense to the local landlords of your space is spiritual feng shui at its easiest.

There are many ways to offer incense to the cosmic spirits. In temples, they use joss sticks, and just lighting a single stick of incense, when done with thoughts of reverence, are incredibly powerful!

For spiritual feng shui purposes, we prefer to offer incense by burning specific incense known to be "favoured" by the local spirits. To dispel obstacles and interferences to success, burn dark incense such as agrawood or gugul. To attract good fortune and the support of higher cosmic Deities such as the **Earth Goddesses**, burn incense made from light coloured wood such as **frankincense** or **sandalwood** (which is actually golden).

There are incredible benefits to burning incense around the outside space of your home. Whether you live in a landed house or in an apartment, incense purifies and cleanses your space. Carry your **incense burner** from room to room, moving round each of the rooms three times in a clockwise direction. Done once a week on your **Day of Obstacles** which is **Tuesday**, the incense clears away all negativity and cleanses your home of bad energy.

You can offer incense at any time but we prefer to do it after the sun has set – anytime from **7pm onwards**. We usually use the conveniently mixed instant incense pellets that burn easily. These are clean and emit an amazing fragrance, neither too sweet nor excessively pungent. Use an incense burner with a handle. As you light the incense, recite prayers to consecrate the incense with this incantation mantra, recited 21 times:

NAMAH SARVA TATHAGATA AVALOKITE OM SAMBHARA SAMBHARA HUNG

Then think that you are making offering of the incense to the Earth Goddess, Sky Gods, local landlords and protectors in and around your house, your street and your neighbourhood. You can think that they are accepting the incense and then you can even request for a specific illness or obstacle to be removed.

PART SIX

MONKEY LIVING IN EIGHT DIRECTION HOUSES

The Effect of Facing & Sitting Axis Directions on Monkey's Luck in 2013

The Eight Direction Houses theory of feng shui contends that depending on whether you are an EAST or WEST person, different "axis" directions are more suitable for you. Whether your house is auspicious for you or not depends very much on this axis direction, comprising both sitting and facing direction.

It is not always easy to determine these directions accurately, and this is a very crucial point to get right when arranging the feng shui of your house.

Often, to determine these directions accurately requires onsite investigations. However, as a general guide, we can say that it is easier to start by determining the facing direction of the house, following which, the opposite of the facing direction is then deemed to be the sitting direction. Thus the facing direction is the direct opposite of the sitting direction.

For general purposes, here are the important guidelines you may want to take note of to determine the facing direction of your house (here please be careful to note that the facing direction of your front door is not always the same as the facing direction of your house, although in terms of feng shui, it is always more auspicious for the two directions to be the same).

For landed properties, the facing direction is considered to be the direction or orientation receiving maximum yang chi, which can be a view of the city, a big or main road, or a market, a bright open space or where lots of people congregate. The orientation design should also be taken into account i.e. how the front of the building is built to "face" this source of yang chi.

Usually, there should also be an opening into the house so that the yang chi is then able to flow seamlessly into the home. When this yang chi is coming from one of your personalized lucky directions, then the house is lucky for you!

 For apartments and condominiums, the facing direction is usually also the source of maximum yang chi entering into your apartment. This is considered to be the largest living room window or patio opening. There can be a glass door so the view is visible. Yang energy thus "flows" into the apartment from here. This direction is then considered to be the "facing direction" of the apartment. If there is no large window, then the biggest "window opening" can be regarded as the facing direction. Definitely it is not the door into the apartment, which either faces a corridor or the lift shaft.

Apartments below the 9th floor can also **use the entire apartment building to determine their facing direction** and this means looking for the facing direction of the whole apartment building. If this entrance into the building is auspicious for you, then your apartment is considered to be lucky for you, especially if it is also located in a sector of the building that corresponds to one of your personal lucky directions.

AUSPICIOUS DIRECTIONS
for Monkey Men

AGE IN 2013 OF DIFFERENT MONKEY YEARS	EAST/WEST GROUP	LUCKY FACING OR SITTING DIRECTIONS
WOOD MONKEY/ 69 YEARS	WEST	NE, WEST, NW, SW
FIRE MONKEY/ 57 YEARS	WEST	SW, NW, WEST, NE
EARTH MONKEY/ 45 YEARS	WEST	NE, WEST, NW, SW
METAL MONKEY/ 33 YEARS	WEST	NE, WEST, NW, SW
WATER MONKEY/ 21 YEARS	WEST	SW, NW, WEST, NE
WOOD MONKEY/ 9 YEARS	WEST	NE, WEST, NW, SW

AUSPICIOUS DIRECTIONS
for Monkey Women

AGE IN 2013 OF DIFFERENT MONKEY YEARS	EAST/WEST GROUP	LUCKY FACING OR SITTING DIRECTIONS
WOOD MONKEY/ 69 YEARS	EAST	NORTH, SOUTH, EAST, SE
FIRE MONKEY/ 57 YEARS	WEST	NW, SW, NE, WEST
EARTH MONKEY/ 45 YEARS	EAST	SE, EAST, NORTH, SOUTH
METAL MONKEY/ 33 YEARS	EAST	NORTH, SOUTH, EAST, SE
WATER MONKEY/ 21 YEARS	WEST	NW, SW, NE, WEST
WOOD MONKEY/ 9 YEARS	EAST	SE, EAST, NORTH, SOUTH

Living in a North-South Axis House

The Axis direction means the alignment of the house from front to back, and each group has a specific axis direction that is extra beneficial for them. Thus all East group people benefit from the **North/South** Axis direction because both North and South are directions belonging to the East group. If you are an East person living in a North/South house, it will be very auspicious for you.

Monkey men and women who belong to the East group will discover that living in a house with a North/South axis direction benefits them very much in 2013, and this is because the facing and sitting directions of the house both enjoy auspicious star numbers in 2013 that also add up to ten this year. You can check from the tables to see if the North/South axis benefits you.

Living in a Southwest-Northeast Axis House

For the Monkey-born belonging to the WEST group, living in a **Southwest/Northeast** axis direction house would be very beneficial, especially during this current period of 8 when both Southwest and Northeast are incredibly auspicious.

In fact, **anyone at all** will benefit from living in such houses during the **current period of 8**, which lasts until 2024. East group people also benefit from these directions, even though they are West group directions. This is because houses that face Northeast or Southwest enjoy very special feng shui alignments that bring success and great abundance, especially when water is placed at the front of the house to signify enhancing growth chi.

Note that both the **Southwest** and **Northeast** are West group directions, so anyone belonging to the West group is sure to benefit from houses that have this alignment. For some of you Monkey men and women, the Southwest and Northeast may not directly bring you Success Luck; nevertheless, either direction would be beneficial for you in 2013 and through the entire period of 8.

Living in an East-West or a Southeast-Northwest Axis House

AAs for the other remaining two axis directions, these have an East-facing and a West-sitting axis (or vice versa) and this means that anyone staying in such houses can benefit only from either their facing or their sitting direction, but not both. This does not mean that such houses are less auspicious, as tapping into a compatible facing or sitting direction is already extremely favourable. Also, you can choose a bedroom located in one of your lucky sectors.

Note however that EAST/WEST direction axis houses are excellent in circumstances where the husband and wife belong to different direction groups. Thus if you belong to West group and your spouse belongs to East group, then both of you will benefit from living in the house!

This is one of the best ways of dealing with this sticky problem where each spouse (not to mention the children) have different lucky directions.

It is always most beneficial to **select a house that faces a direction that corresponds to your Success**

direction i.e. the *sheng chi* that brings overall growth luck. This means that the longer you stay in the house, the more prosperous and auspicious you will be.

> When your house faces your sheng chi direction and you energize this with the presence of a pool or pond of yang water, your feng shui becomes extremely good.

Whatever direction your house faces, it always benefits from having water at the front. This is because according to the Eight Mansions theory of feng shui, the growth chi in all "mansions" irrespective of their facing direction is always concentrated at the front foyer area, both inside and outside the house. If possible, it benefits to have some water accumulation (i.e. a pond or a pool) just outside the house in front, and if there is also a door here, it would be most beneficial.

Note that for all **Monkey-born**, regardless of whether you are East or West group, a house facing or sitting in the **Southwest** direction has one added benefit for you, simply because the Southwest is the natural home location of the Monkey (and the compass home locations of all animal signs override the Eight

Mansions formula.) Hence note that even if you are an EAST group Monkey, a house facing Southwest 3 brings incredibly auspicious luck for you. Remember that all **Southwest/Northeast** axis houses also benefit all its residents within the home. Such houses enjoy extraordinary feng shui alignments and auspicious stars in the Period of 8 and are thus considered quite special.

Whatever direction your house faces, according to Eight Mansions feng shui, it is very auspicious to have a small water accumulation such as a pond or pool just outside your front door.

DOOR GUARDIANS FOR 2013
Appeasing the Nagas

The Snake Year is a year when the spirit of the NAGA can be very strong and the key to having a safe and affliction-free year is to appease them. This is usually done by offering a pungent-type incense once a week.

The offering of aromatic fragrance using the fire medium has always been a popular ritual observed by many Eastern and Asian traditions. It is also very popular amongst mountain dwellers. Earth naga spirits abound in mountains!

For convenience, you can offer just one stick of incense daily and this goes a long way to appeasing the naga spirits around your home.

But it is also extremely beneficial to place a pair of **Door Protector Guardians** flanking the entrance into your house.

On landed properties, the door guardians should be placed on floor level on both sides of the main door, outside. **In condominiums or entrances into offices,** the door guardians should also be placed flanking the main entrance on the outside, rather than flanking any large picture window that represents the facing direction

inside. Door guardians are always more efficient when displayed outside rather than inside the house. Those living in homes with more than one entrance can place protector guardians on all the other doors.

In feng shui, we like to use ceramic, wood or brass images of the powerful celestial guardians such as the **Pi Yao** (also known as Pi Kans), the **Chi Lins** and the **Fu Dogs** to guard our doorways, but sometimes these can be excessively "strong" and their presence (especially when they are too large) can be unnecessarily intimidating. So unless you are living in a very dangerous neighborhood, it is advisable to finetune your placement of guardian protectors according to the energies of the year.

This means placing protector guardians according to the facing direction of the door, which in every year is influenced by different energies.

DOORS FACING SOUTHEAST benefit from having a pair of benevolent looking **PI YAO** which can be made of ceramics or carved out of a good variety of fragrant or hard wood is to be preferred. This is because the Southeast is a Wood element direction. Do not place metal Pi Yao in this facing direction.

DOORS FACING SOUTHWEST can be guarded by a pair of **DEER**, especially if made of brass. This would be extremely suitable in 2013 as the Metal energy would suppress the illness star coming from the Southwest direction, and the Deer imagery will bring good health and long life. This is particularly beneficial for all of you born in the year of the Monkey, as well anyone in the house who is a Sheep-born.

DOORS FACING WEST should ideally be guarded by a pair of **ELEPHANTS**. In 2013, energy coming from the West is badly afflicted by violent chi, which also brings betrayal and burglary luck. To suppress this afflictive energy, the powerful elephants would be ideal, especially if you can find elephants that have their trunks raised, and if possible, decorated in blue or Water element motifs. Elephants are always associated with power and strength, and this is suitable for protecting your West direction

DOORS FACING EAST must be protected against the number 3 hostility star, which also brings disharmony, and in extreme cases, legal problems. Energy coming from this direction causes misunderstandings to break out amongst residents, and also quarrels with outsiders, which can be unpleasant and aggravating. To guard against this, get a pair of **PEACOCKS** and place them flanking your door. Better yet if they can be made of brass or some other metal, as this will efficiently take care of whatever quarrelsome energy inadvertently makes its way into your house.

DOORS FACING NORTHEAST benefit from the incoming auspicious 8 energy in 2013, and to welcome this powerfully strong wealth-bringing chi, it is an excellent idea to place a pair of beautifully-decorated **3**

LEGGED TOADS, one on each side of your door. Three legged toads are traditionally regarded as being extremely effective for drawing in auspicious wealth-bringing energy into homes

DOORS FACING SOUTH benefit from the completion star of 9, and the essence of Fire energy is best symbolized by the **HORSE,** the creature always associated with the South. Thus placing a pair of horses here in 2013 would be excellent. The horse can also signify the powerful Wind Horse if made in the correct pose with the Wind Horse mantra and carrying the wish fulfilling jewel on its back. Best made out of ceramic or wood.

DOORS FACING NORTH Here, the best protection is brought by the popular **DRAGON TORTOISE.** The Tortoise is the celestial symbol of protection and support of the North, and placing a pair here will also activate the chi energy of victory.

DOORS FACING NORTHWEST will benefit from having a pair of **WINGED CHI LIN** which is the Dragon-headed Horse. The Northwest is the direction from which heavenly chi wafts into the home. In 2013, heavenly chi comes from this direction, and the winged Chi Lin directs such energy effectively into the home. Best if the images are made of ceramic.

So... Are You Ready?

Did you enjoy this book and gain some meaningful insights about your own animal sign and personal fortune? If you use this book properly and as I have instructed, it is a goldmine of feng shui knowledge that will yield great good fortune to you. But you must take action... nothing will happen if you do not take action and move forward.

And With Your Permission...

I'd like to send you absolutely FREE, my weekly news and updates. You'll learn even more of my secrets, which will open your mind to the deeper possibilities of feng shui today.

Lillian Too's FREE online weekly newsletter is now AVAILABLE in SPANISH and in ENGLISH.

Here's how easy it is to join!
Just go online to *www.liliantoomandalaezine.com* for the ENGLISH version, or *www.lamandaladelilliantoo.com* for the SPANISH VERSION and sign up today.

Your newsletter will automatically be delivered to your inbox every week… and if you find this information is not what you need or want you can unsubscribe easily.

....

But it's only available to those who register online at:
www.lilliantoomandalaezine.com

....

And everyone who receives my FREE weekly newsletter is eligible for special discounts, unadvertised offers and early bird specials!

DON'T BE LEFT OUT!
JOIN US TODAY!

And thanks again for investing in yourself and the ancient knowledge of feng shui. Now join me every week and learn how you can easily and quickly change your life for the better.

Lillian Too's online FREE weekly ezine (newsletter) is only available when you register online at
www.lilliantoomandalaezine.com